CALVIN COOLIDGE

HIS IDEALS OF CITIZENSHIP

AS REVEALED THROUGH HIS SPEECHES AND WRITINGS

BY

EDWARD ELWELL WHITING

W. A. WILDE COMPANY

BOSTON MASSACHUSETTS

1924

ACKNOWLEDGMENT

AUTHOR and publishers unite in acknowledging their appreciation to J. E. Purdy of Boston for the use of the frontispiece, to Houghton Mifflin Company and Charles Scribner's Sons for permission to make liberal quotations from "Have Faith in Massachusetts" and "The Price of Freedom" respectively.

AUTHOR'S FOREWORD

The character of Calvin Coolidge is best revealed by his own words. To understand his attitude towards matters of public policy and government, and to forecast with a reasonable degree of accuracy his probable action in future events, it is necessary to go to his public papers and addresses. In these may be found indication of a definite political philosophy.

The careers of public men sometimes are shaped by events alone. Sometimes they are determined by a definite policy of expediency. Sometimes they find their motive in an intense personal ambition. Sometimes they are controlled by considerations of selfish aggrandizement. In the case of Calvin Coolidge none of these forces operate. The framework of his public career stands upon the firm foundation of early-formed moral principles.

Many men have sought to analyze his character. The clearest analysis is the unconscious

7

self-analysis contained in his own utterances.
Mr. Coolidge is not introspective. He does not
spend time examining his own motives. He
has no sense of ego. He gives no sign of concern
for what others may think of his actions, except
in so far as he has due regard for the respect and
confidence of those in whose principles he
believes and upon whose honesty he relies.

What Mr. Coolidge's own words show is in no
sense or degree a conscious self-study. There
is no trace of that in anything he has ever said or
written. He has no taint of self-consciousness.
What we find in his words is rather a subcon-
scious reflection of those essential principles
which are the heart of his nature. To a large
degree Mr. Coolidge's principles are instinctive.
To a lesser degree they are the result of cold
thought keyed in an extraordinary capacity for
sane judgment. This carefully calculated development by Mr. Coolidge of his own qualities
has produced a character in public life incom-
prehensible to some, yet easily comprehended.
It enables one who knows him to trace through
his self-expression as contained in his papers

and speeches the reason by which he directs his actions.

Those who have read some or all of his words have for the most part gained some sense of the man's nature. All have gained an impression of his forcefulness of utterance and his clarity of thinking. Some have discovered that substantial political philosophy which distinguishes him among his contemporaries and which arouses comparisons with the statesmen of preceding eras. It is the purpose of this book to guide those who wish to know Coolidge through the avenues which he himself has charted.

History shows that great men do not suffer changes in character. Greatness is not acquired; it is but developed or revealed. When a man achieves eminence, the public likes to look back over the record of his life. Sometimes in doing so we bring forth anecdotes indicative of early aspirations or illustrative of early tendencies later to be fulfilled and justified. That revealment of a man's youth which has to do with the operations of his mind rather than with his specific actions is the more important and the less frequent. Many anecdotes of Mr. Coolidge's youth have been told. They are interesting. Anecdotes of the youth of great men always interest. In the case of Mr. Coolidge we have available, however, something more important and something more convincing than stories of his early performances. We have his writings. They are the key to Coolidge.

Mr. Coolidge has been many years in public life. He is a politician, using the word in its correct sense. He has described politics as "the art of government." He entered active political life before he had established a career in other lines. Admitted to the bar, he early elected to concern himself with matters of government. He made his choice as a young man. He was not drafted from the law to the State House. He did not seek escape from his profession by means of political adventure. His choice was deliberate. It was based on calculation — not a calculation of possible rewards to come, but a calculation of his preference in life. That preference lay in the public service of politics and government. Since making that decision he has held many offices. He has never been defeated when a candidate for office. He has never aggressively sought an office; the suggestion of his candidacy has invariably come from outside the dictates of personal ambition. He was city solicitor in Northampton, Massachusetts. He has been the mayor of that city. He has served in both branches of the Massachusetts legislature. He served two terms as president of his state senate. He has been lieutenant governor and governor of Massachusetts. He has been vice president. He is the President.

Throughout these years of public service he has been modest and humble. He has not sought self-advertising. In his address to the state senate on one occasion he used these words: "Do the day's work." This has been quoted as his motto. He has never said it was his motto. He is not a man who follows formulas of that sort. Yet those words express as well as any could his method of service. He does the day's work. In doing so, he has had occasion to make many addresses, both as an official of

government and as a political candidate. He
has had occasion to prepare papers and articles.
These cover the years of his public career to
date. They reach even to his college days. It
is in these papers and addresses that we find the
guide to Coolidge.

For the casual reader to undertake by a study
of Mr. Coolidge's own words to reach a complete comprehension of his political character,
and thereby to feel able to gauge his probable
course of action in relation to public matters,
would require much time and effort. The
reader making this undertaking would face the
necessity of tracing through many discussions
of specific matters the thread by which, and
by which alone, one may arrive at the motivating factor in the man. Having read substan-
tially all of his writings and speeches, the reader
would then feel impelled to read them again in
the effort to pick up the thread lost in the confusion incidental to so large a mass of material.

Familiarity with Mr. Coolidge's writings and
with his career establishes the conviction that
there is in fact such a definite thread running

throughout the whole fabric of his relation to
government. It is with the purpose of following that thread and indicating its source that
this book has been prepared. We have sought
by examination of his writings and speeches,
supplemented by admiration for and some
knowledge of the man himself, to make such
selections, and so to connect them, as to make
clear to the reader exactly what springs operate
the mind of President Coolidge.

It will be found that here is a mentally consistent man. It will be found that he sees
government clearly because he sees it simply.
A study of him in this manner, utilizing his own
words rather than enlisting the opinions of
others, should perform two services: One, the
revealment of the mental processes of a statesman; two, emphasis upon the essential simplicity of government.

We are all inclined to erect in our thoughts
a vast and complicated structure which we call
government. As laymen we stand in awe before
it, or we dismiss it as something incomprehen-
sible and possibly uninteresting. Any study of

Mr. Coolidge, through his own words, should reveal the important fact that government is in fact simple and comprehensible in all of its essential parts. An examination of Mr. Coolidge's mind, and through it a vision of government as he sees it, should go far to increase popular comprehension of democracy.

That republic will prosper best which has the largest degree of understanding and coöperation from those who live as a part of it. Calvin Coolidge has done more than any statesman in many years to make possible a popular understanding of government and to encourage the coöperation which is most desired.

We present in the following chapters the political philosophy and faith of Calvin Coolidge as revealed by himself. His standards of citizenship are set forth in his own words. The thought behind the President is presented for Americans to understand.

We have here sought by a process of selection and condensation to present in one volume a moral conception of government by a statesman whose guide it is.

TABLE OF CONTENTS

15

16 TABLE OF CONTENTS

CALVIN COOLIDGE

HIS IDEALS OF CITIZENSHIP

CHAPTER I

THE MEANING OF DEMOCRACY

Calvin Coolidge sees democracy as an essentially positive creation. He has no picture of it as simply a negation of something else, or as a departure from preceding forms of government. In an address which he delivered July 4, 1916, at the home of Daniel Webster in Marshfield, Massachusetts, he said:

"Democracy is not a tearing-down; it is a building-up. It is not a denial of the divine right of kings; it supplements that claim with the assertion of the divine right of all men. It does not destroy; it fulfills. It is the consummation of all theories of government, to the spirit of which all the nations of the earth must yield. It is the great constructive force of the ages. It is the alpha and omega of man's rela-

17

tion to man, the beginning and the end. There is and can be no more doubt of the triumph of democracy in human affairs, than there is of the triumph of gravitation in the physical world; the only question is how and when. Its foundation lays hold upon eternity."

The foundation upon which Mr. Coolidge rests that faith in democracy which is expressed above, is formed from his study and examination of other and older theories of government. The point which he emphasizes time and again in his writings and addresses is well summed up in his assertion that "Democracy is not a tearing-down; it is a building-up." He sees democracy making a positive contribution to the achievements of the human race. He believes, as we understand by his references to this subject, in the permanency of the central principles of self-government among peoples. He emphasizes frequently the thought that democracy is not simply a bridge, but is, on the contrary, a permanent political and moral force, and that as such it must forever dominate the thoughts of mankind; its authority is increasing proportionately with the development of human education. "Its foundation," he says, "lays hold upon eternity."

In a talk before the Evanston Sunday Afternoon Club at Evanston, Illinois, on January 21, 1923, he developed the distinguishing differences between class governments and democracy. In that address he emphasized the stimulating effect of self-government upon those who sincerely practice it.   Mr. Coolidge does not see in this form of government an appeal to ease or a refuge for the slothful.   It is a characteristic of many of his addresses to insist upon the exacting requirements of such a government as ours.   That thought, so characteristic of him, appears clearly in the Evanston address.   We make liberal quotation from it because of its significance and because, also, of the recentness of its utterance.   He was then vice president of the United States and had had the experience of nearly two years close to the center of national government in Washington.   In that address he referred to "two broad theories which have held sway in the world," and proceeded:

"There are two broad theories which have held sway in the world. They have developed with the development of the race. One is the system of class and caste, the system of servitude of body and of mind, of a claim of divine right of rulers by inheritance — a system where the individual is nothing and the government is all supreme. . . .

"There is another system with which every American should be familiar, a system of equality and of freedom, not without the claim of divine right, but recognizing that such right reposes in the people; a system where the individual is clothed with inalienable rights, the people are supreme, the government is their agent. Under this conception there is real freedom, real independence, and grave personal responsibility. The rulers look to the people. Their authority is the public will, ascertained in accordance with law. There will be the least possible interference with private affairs. Realizing that it is the people who support the government and not the government which supports the people, there will be no resort to paternalism. Under such institutions there may appear to be a lack of machine-like efficiency, but there will be no lack of character. Private initiative will be stimulated. Self-reliance and self-control will be increased. Society will remain a living organism sustaining hope and progress, content to extend its dominion not by conquest but by service. Such is the system of self-government, the orderly rule of the people, carrying within itself a remedy for its own disorders and the power of self-perpetuation. This is the ideal of America.

"No one would say that existence under these conditions is effortless. Independence is exceedingly exacting, self-control is arduous, self-government is difficult. Always there is the temptation that some element of these should be surrendered in exchange for security and ease. The appeal to passion and prejudice always lies in this direction. The proposal to despoil others of their possessions is a manifestation of the same spirit. This is the reason that to certain of our native-born, and more often to our foreign-born, the American Repub-

lic proves a disappointment. They thought
that self-government meant the absence of all
restraint, that independence meant living without work, and that freedom was the privilege of
doing what they wanted to do. It has been a
hard lesson for them to learn that self-government is still government, that the rule of the
people does not mean absence of authority,
that independence means self-support, and that
complete freedom means complete obedience to
law. They are disappointed more than ever
when they learn, as ever they do, that these are
so, not because they have been decreed by some
body of men, but that they are so by the very
nature of things, and all the governments in
the world are powerless to change them.

"Here again it is perfectly obvious that if
the American system is to be cast aside there
is only the one other system which can be
adopted. The call of the old life of ignorance,
of fear, of superstition, of every savage instinct
is all toward the old system. The call of the
new life of learning, of courage, of enlightened
reason, of faith, of religion, is all toward the new

system. In a contest between these forces it
does not seem difficult to judge which are finally
to be supreme."

The discriminating will find in his words an
inspiring summons. He preaches here, as else-
where, the doctrine of effort. He is in this
address, as in many others, an apostle for the
strenuous life applied to the practices of self-
government — not the strenuous life of physical
activity but that of mental and moral perceptions requisite for any true comprehension of
America. Some unfamiliar with Mr. Coolidge's
political creed have failed to grasp an essential
fact in his character, which is set forth far better
in his own writings than can be done by any one,
however well disposed, who undertakes to de-
scribe him to others. This fact is that he has a
keen sympathy for humanity, and a very clear
understanding of the fallibility of human procedure. A glimpse of this attitude appears above
in his observation that "under such institutions
there may appear to be a lack of machine-like
efficiency, but there will be no lack of character. . . . Self-reliance and self-control will be

increased. Society will remain a living organism."

Mr. Coolidge in all his utterances faces the future with confidence. "The call of the new life of learning, of courage, of enlightened reason, of faith, of religion, is all toward the new system."

Mr. Coolidge constantly sees the element of necessary effort in all who live under self-government; he sees this both as a virtue and as an attraction — never as a liability. It is a favorite theme with him. The reader as he goes through the succeeding chapters of this book will find him repeatedly emphasizing it. Mr. Coolidge's Americanism contains no counsel of soft ways and evasions.

In an address delivered February 22, 1922, at Johns Hopkins University, taking as his text George Washington, he said :

"The meaning of America is not to be found in a life without toil. Freedom is not only bought with a great price; it is maintained by unremitting effort. The successful conduct of our economic life is not easy. It cannot be made easy. The burdens of existence, the

weight of civilization, cannot be taken from the
people.   There is no way to establish a better
relationship among the people of this nation
save through each making great sacrifice.   But
nowhere does duty done and sacrifice made hold
the promise of larger success.   The final solution of these problems will not be found in the
interposition of government in all the affairs
of the people, but rather in following the wisdom
of Washington, who refused to exercise authority over the people, that the people might
exercise authority over themselves.   It is not in
the laying on of force, but in the development
of the public conscience that salvation lies."

In that address as in others he presents the
thought that our American form of representative democracy is not a device for the removal
of responsibility from the shoulders of the
people, but is, on the contrary, a method that
inevitably places the responsibility there.   He
does not see our government as designed to
lighten the burdens of the people in the sense
that they need not give thought or effort to
their political problems; our government is

a process in which success depends always upon
the will, courage, and effort of the people. But
he sees and points out that such burdens as
democracy imposes upon us are those which
all normal persons delight to bear. They are
distinguishable from such burdens as are expressed in the oppressions inevitable under a
despotism. Self-government imposes burdens
but does not oppress. "It is not in the laying
on of force, but in the development of the public
conscience that salvation lies."

Mr. Coolidge holds no brief, however, for such
negation of government authority as might
follow the practice of democracy unchecked
by the representative system which has always
obtained in the United States. The authority
of government remains constant and, responsive to the enlightened will of the people, may be
called upon and relied upon to correct abuses,
and to restore or revitalize liberties placed in
jeopardy. This thought he expressed in an
address January 11, 1922, before the Hamilton
Club at Chicago on the anniversary of the birthday of Alexander Hamilton:

"There came a time at the beginning of this century when economic freedom was threatened, when great combinations were gaining the power to control the business life of the nation and extending an undue influence over the affairs of the government itself. The open door of opportunity, which had always been the American ideal, was in danger of being closed. Through the enactment of new laws, but more especially through the administration and enforcement of old laws, that danger and that threat were averted. Government control and regulation are still new. They have at times been mistakenly applied. They will need the modification which experience shall demonstrate both of withdrawal and advance; but they have kept open the door, they have reëstablished freedom. This was . . . the application of the theory of Hamilton to present conditions, that the government have and use the power necessary for the economic welfare of the country."

It will not pass unobserved that in thus exercising Hamilton's theory that the government have and use the powers necessary for the economical welfare of the country, Mr. Coolidge's thought was still consistently centered upon the essentially democratic nature of our country, and that he had in mind the basic necessity for preserving the economic freedom of the nation.

As we go onward through the exhibit of Mr. Coolidge's thought as expressed by him on many occasions, covering many years, we shall find reiterated his clear understanding of the ultimate responsibility and the ultimate authority of the people themselves. It will be seen from his words that he has a sense of the inevitability of self-government. So long ago as 1895, when Calvin Coolidge was a senior at Amherst College, he possessed this lively sense of democratic verity. At that time the Sons of the American Revolution offered a prize of a gold medal for the best essay on "The Causes of the American Revolution." This contest was open to the seniors of colleges and universities throughout this country. Mr. Coolidge's essay won for him the medal. In that essay he said:

"Sovereignty is always finally vested in the people. It may need a theocracy to lead a people out of barbarism; this may develop into a despotism with the power divided between kings and bishops; but a struggle is sure to come, and the people will gather about the king to make him a monarch, like Louis XIV, who really was an objective realization of the state. This, too, will be but temporary; the people will realize more and more that the sovereignty is with them and will finally assert it."

Mr. Coolidge's conception of the meaning of democracy is one in which the people are sovereigns in the fullest sense. He sees them not as receivers of bounty, not as the easy-going objects of paternalism, but as vital factors in working out the problems of perfecting civilization. Throughout his public life he has taken occasion at almost every opportunity to stir the minds of the people toward a constructive assertiveness. "I sometimes wish," he said on April 11, 1924, in a brief address to the members of the Women's National Committee for Law Enforcement, "that people would put a little more emphasis on the observance of the law than they do on its enforcement. It is a maxim of our institutions that the government does not make the people, but the people make the government."

Under Mr. Coolidge's conception of the meaning of democracy it is not a gift from some mysterious source to the people; nor is it a gift of authority from the people to a governing unit; it is essentially an identification of people and government. Thus, all government problems are the people's problems; all that inures to the benefit of the people creates vitality in government.

CHAPTER II

The Authority of Government

Calvin Coolidge has an abiding faith in the American people. This he has expressed in frequent phrase. This he has demonstrated by a consistent course. He trusts the people, and so trusting them, he has no fears for the durability of self-government. He knows, as all men who have been close to the heart of government know, that where power exists, power will be used. He knows that in electing a government, that government will function in response to conditions about it. Mr. Coolidge's respect for the institution of government is an essential part of his faith in the people. Affiliated with a political party, he sees partisanship as one of the necessary factors in government, but not as an end toward which all things proceed. He knows that there are crises in which the basic principles of representative government transcend in importance all other considerations.

This high regard for government, this dignified conception of its responsibility, he set forth in a speech February 13, 1924. The country then was in the midst of most disturbing revelations brought forth by investigations conducted by certain senate committees. In this speech of February 13 he lifted the issue away from the low plain of partisanship. "Character," he said, "is the only secure foundation of the state." He continued :

"Character is the only secure foundation of the state. We know well that all plans for improving the machinery of government and all measures for social betterment miserably fail, and the hopes of progress wither, when corruption touches administration. At the revelation of greed making its subtle approaches to public officers, of the prostitution of high place to private profit, we are filled with scorn and indignation. We have a deep sense of humiliation at such gross betrayal of trust, and we lament the undermining of public confidence in official integrity. But we cannot rest with righteous wrath; still less can we permit ourselves to give way to cynicism. The heart of the American people is sound. Their officers with rare exception are faithful and high-minded. For us, we propose to follow the clear, open path of justice. There will be immediate, adequate, unshrinking prosecution, criminal and civil, to punish the guilty and to protect every national interest. In this effort there will be no politics, no partisanship. It will be speedy, it will be just. I am a Republican but I cannot on that account shield any one because he is a Republican. I am a Republican, but I cannot on that account prosecute any one because he is a Democrat. . . .

"Distressing as this situation has been, it has its reassuring side. The high moral standards of the people were revealed by their instant reaction against wrongdoing."

Here again we find expressed his ineradicable faith in America. "The heart of the American people is sound." And again, "The high moral standards of the people were revealed by their instant reaction against wrongdoing."

It is not, however, in such situations that the peril to representative democracy is most dangerous. "The greatest peril to our institutions," said Mr. Coolidge, in an address before the Women's Roosevelt Memorial Association at New York on January 23, 1921, "does not lie in a direct assault upon them, nor will it come from those who, with evil intent, strive for their destruction. Disaster will come from those who probably with good intentions seek the private control of public action."

That quotation is of particular interest in its bearing upon the quotation preceding it. When Mr. Coolidge pointed to the peril to our institutions from the effort of private control over public action, even though with possibly good intentions, he had not then taken office as vice president of the United States, to which he had been elected in the preceding November. Moralists have written and spoken at much length concerning all phases of those matters agitated during the senate committee hearings. There certainly was indicated in many of the facts then brought forth an effort to exert private

control of public action. Omitting all reference
to proved or alleged corruption, there remains
for consideration the pernicious potentialities
of those who possibly with good intentions did
seek by private agencies to direct the course
of public action. We may regard Mr. Coolidge's
words of January, 1921, as in some measure
prophetic.

The authority of government is imperiled
not only by the open enemies of our system of
government, and not only by those who seek
the private control of public action, with possibly
good intentions, but also by many who are
utterly unselfish, but who mistakenly, or in a
sort of panic, counsel ways which are insidiously
destructive. This peril to our institutions Mr.
Coolidge dealt with in an address delivered
April 18, 1923, at Boston, in celebration of the
two hundredth anniversary of Christ Church —
better known as the Old North Church. In
that address he said:

"There are voices which are counseling the
destruction of the rights of the individual which
our institutions were established to maintain,

some by out-and-out revolution. But these
need only to be brought into the light of publicity to wither away. There are others which
are more insidious, more dangerous, which
come under the guise of government activity
instigated for the general good. Our fathers
sought for an enlarged freedom, for the right
to enjoy the rewards of their own industry.
They had felt the oppression of government
regulation, competition, and monopoly. They
wished to be rid of these restrictions. That
most precious privilege they gained. They
can maintain it only upon one condition, that
they use it righteously. It is the abuse of liberty
which warrants oppression. If the people will
pursue a course of economic and industrial
righteousness, there will be no motive for inter-
fering with their liberty by drastic government
regulation, or sequestration of their property
by government operation, or a confiscation of
the results of their industry in the name of
taxation. It is the existence of a wrong public
sentiment, a wrong standard, whether expressed
in private economic relations or in government

attempt to remedy what cannot be remedied by law, which causes the evil. In either case, there is a harmful curtailment of freedom."

In those words we again have a glimpse of Mr. Coolidge's accurate perception of the community of interests between the people of a republic and their agencies of government. The privilege which our forefathers established for us we "can maintain only upon one condition," that we use it righteously. He points out that it is the abuse of liberty which warrants oppression. This sentence sums up the most insidious menace to our liberties and to our institutions : "It is the existence of a wrong public sentiment, a wrong standard, whether expressed in private economic relations or in government attempt to remedy what cannot be remedied by law, which causes the evil." His conclusion is that in either case "there is a harmful curtailment of freedom."

The delicate balance inseparable from a sensitive representative form of government is manifested by the mutual effect upon government processes and the people as a whole caused

by the unwisdom of either. When by a series
of economic selfishnesses there is forced drastic
governmental action; by so much is the principle of individual liberty jeopardized. When
by an assertion of arrogance on the part of
office-proud politicians the rights of the public
are transgressed, then there is fanned a spirit
of discontent which may become a serious
menace, first to that respect which is requisite
for the maintenance of free institutions, and,
second, to the stability of those institutions
themselves.

Mr. Coolidge in many of his addresses has
evinced his high regard for the authority of
government as such. He sees in the forms of
a government manifestation of the authority
of representative democracy.

CHAPTER III

American Respect for Law

Calvin Coolidge first came into national prominence associated with the issue of law and
order. It was the incident of the Boston police
strike which focused the country's attention
upon him. This was an incident of history;
it was also an incident, and no more than an
incident, in his career. It was, moreover, only
an incidental manifestation of a quality in the
man which is constant. All that Mr. Coolidge
said and did as Governor of Massachusetts,
when a large proportion of the Boston police
left their posts, is in precise accord with what
may be called his permanent attitude toward
law. The large degree of success which attended his course in that crisis, the overwhelming
national approval of what he said in his public
utterances at that time, indicate the fact that
Mr. Coolidge accurately appraises always the

essential American respect for law. Throughout his writings and speaking, during many
years in public life, we find repeated manifestations not only of his own regard for law and
the principles of American democracy, whose
aim is liberty under law, but also equally important manifestations of the accuracy with
which he reads the heart of his countrymen and
the thoroughness with which he trusts their
instincts and their conscience. Much of the
stability of America rests on the firm foundation of respect for law.   Much of Mr. Coolidge's
success in politics rests upon his unwavering
faith in that respect.   " The heart of the American people is sound."   He knows this to be true.
The knowledge gives him authority.

When Mr. Coolidge said in his telegram of
September 14, 1919, addressed to Samuel Gom-
pers, "There is no right to strike against the
public safety by anybody, anywhere, any time,"
he knew that the thought in those words was
at the very base of American character. It
coincided with American respect for law. In
this same telegram he said : "I wish to join and

assist in taking a broad view of every situation. A grave responsibility rests on all of us. You can depend on me to support you in every legal action and sound policy. I am equally determined to defend the sovereignty of Massachusetts and to maintain the authority and jurisdiction over her public officers where it has been placed by the constitution and law of her people." Therein we find manifested again both his own regard for law and his confidence in the determination of the people to proceed, and to support others to proceed, in absolute conformity with the law.

In a proclamation issued by him as Governor on September 24, 1919, when there were apparent difficulties in replacing those members of the police force who had left their posts, Mr. Coolidge said: "I propose to support all those who are supporting their own government with every power which the people have intrusted to me. There is an obligation, inescapable, no less solemn, to resist all those who do not support the government. The authority of the Commonwealth cannot be intimidated or coerced. It cannot be compromised." He closed this proclamation by calling upon every citizen to stand by him in executing the oath of his office and supporting the authority of the government. "This is the cause of the people," he said.

Governor Coolidge's appraisal of the public was correct. That American respect for law which has always sustained the nation now sustained him.

Mr. Coolidge was awarded a gold medal by the National Institute of Social Sciences in recognition of his action in connection with the Boston police strike. In his speech of acceptance, delivered January 23, 1921, at New York, he said : "It is no accident that the people of the Commonwealth of Massachusetts believe in law and order. It is their heritage. When the Pilgrim Fathers landed there in 1620 they brought ashore with them the Mayflower compact, which they had drawn up in the cabin of that little bark under the witness of the Almighty, in which they pledged themselves, one to another, to make just and equitable laws, and not only to make them, but, when they were made, to abide by them. So that, for three hundred years, that has been the policy and the principle of that Commonwealth."

In those words we find a key to the confidence that was his at the time of the police strike, and which was justified by public opinion not only in his own state of Massachusetts but throughout the country. So much has been said about that incident in Boston and in Massachusetts history, and so much emphasis has been placed upon it as a factor in Mr. Coolidge's political progress that it is important, if we are to understand the man, and if we are with reasonable accuracy to gauge his probable course of action at all times, to recognize the fact that there was nothing in connection with the police strike which departed from, or which in any degree amplified, Mr. Coolidge's consistent comprehension both of American government and of the respect of all normal Americans for its essential principles. The police strike merely provided a means of demonstration of a constant quality in the man. He has studied in-

telligently the early history of America. He
has weighed correctly the contribution which
the Pilgrim Fathers made when they drew up
the Mayflower compact and so set permanently
the measure of American respect for law. How
earnestly Mr. Coolidge regards the necessity
for such a respect, nationally held, is set forth
by a few sentences from his address October 31,
1921, at the Convention of the American Legion
in Kansas City, Missouri:

"Government and industry, locality and society, all need the national outlook. . . . It is
time, in every activity in our land, for men in
every relationship to stop trying to get the
better of each other and begin trying to serve
each other. . . .

"The sole guaranty of liberty is obedience to
law under the forms of ordered government.
The observance of the law is the function of
every private citizen, but the execution of the
law is the function only of duly constituted
public authorities."

In those sentences we find a thread of thought
which appears with great frequency throughout

his speeches and writings. It is the thought which yokes and keeps always together in mind the dual responsibility for the maintenance of our form of government. It is the responsibility of the constituted public authorities for the execution of the law, and the equally vital responsibility of every private citizen to observe the law. Much of the hold which Mr. Coolidge has upon the respect of the American people is due to the innate, though often unexpressed, popular recognition of this important fact. Mr. Coolidge always counts upon the American respect for law. It has never failed him.

In one of his addresses he said: "Faith in the people is an American ideal. Not faith in their ignorance or their prejudice."

We find throughout this man's expressions of himself, in the written or spoken word, a firm faith in the people. He has appealed, as will be apparent from quotations thus far made and from others to be made in later chapters, not to the ignorance, prejudice, or passion of the people, but to their intelligence, and, above all, to their respect for law. No thought appears more frequently in his utterances than that. It underlies his whole conception of American democracy.

CHAPTER IV

LAW AND LIBERTY

Mr. Coolidge's writings and speeches show that his veneration for law is uniformly attuned to the thought that law serves liberty. We do not find anywhere in his expression of himself a fanatical or detached worship of law as an abstract and bloodless thing. He sees in law one of the guaranties of human freedom. He frequently expresses the thought that liberty can exist only through the agency of wise laws honestly executed. In his inaugural address as Governor of Massachusetts, January 2, 1919, he said: "Each individual must have the rewards and opportunities worthy of the character of our citizenship, a broader recognition of his worth, and a larger liberty, protected by order — and always under the law."

American respect for law is made possible and permanent not by the intrinsic force of law as an abstraction, but by the American comprehension of the truth that it is the necessary accompaniment of any which can endure.

We may quote at some length from an address by Mr. Coolidge on December 21, 1922, before the County Teachers' Institute and School Directors Convention at Reynoldsville, Pennsylvania:

"There is need of a better understanding of the American form of government. Self-government is still government. There is no such thing as liberty without restraint. My rights are always represented by the duties of others. My freedom is always represented by the obedience of others. Their rights and their freedom are represented by my duties and my obedience. In all the discussion of the American government that has gone on since its establishment, the chief stress and emphasis has been put upon freedom and liberty. The perfecting of human relationships to which our country has made such an enormous contribution has, in a very large degree, lain in that direction. This possession must be defended, supported, and cherished, for it is of priceless value. . . . Any attempt to maintain rights, to secure freedom and liberty for ourselves without the observance of duties and the rendering of obedience toward others, is a contradiction of terms. It defeats itself. . . .

"We are a race of beings created in a universe where law reigns. That will forever need all the repetition and emphasis which can be put on it. Law reigns. It can neither be cheated, evaded, nor turned aside. We can discover it, live in accordance with it, observe it, and develop, and succeed; or, we can disregard it, violate it, defy it, and fail. Law reigns. It is the source of order, of freedom, of righteous authority, of organized society, and also of industrial success and prosperity. To disregard it is to perish, to observe it is to live, physically, mentally, morally, spiritually. It is this principle that requires respect and reverence for authority. It is not sought for the benefit of those who may temporarily represent government or any other example of authority, but for the benefit of the individual himself."

The inexorable laws which order the universe are to Mr. Coolidge a sign placed before humanity for its guidance. Legislation in behalf of human affairs begets what we call law, but which is true law only in so far as it has those aspects of natural truth which distinguish the laws of nations. It is the greater law upon which the existence of the world depends which impresses Mr. Coolidge. "We are a race of beings created in a universe where law reigns." He says the statement needs frequent repetition and emphasis. We may add that it also needs emphasis if we are at all to comprehend the temper of Mr. Coolidge's political philosophy. He is instinctively distrustful of the unnatural in government. He sees government simply, knowing that the essentials of government are simple. Time and again throughout his utterances we find either direct reference to the inexorable laws of the universe or a suggestion of them. As he knows that these universal laws are necessary for the stability of the universe, so he knows that if the human race anywhere at any time is to establish and to preserve liberties, it must do so in accord with sane laws.

We are taught in school to revere the memories of those who fought for American independence. Americans will never falter in their enthusiasm for that epochal achievement in human history. What we sometimes forget, or fail to give due prominence in our thought, is that in anchoring that independence so that it might not slip away from those who had done so much to win it, there was done that which made a nation. Mr. Coolidge calls attention to this anchoring of American independence, in a speech which again exemplifies his insistence upon the unity of liberty and law. He says:

"The foremost achievement of the period was something more than independence. It was the establishment of a nation under the American Constitution. This was the acknowledgment and declaration of the great principle that a larger liberty is to be found in the remission of a lesser freedom. The former colonies gave up their independence, merged their small estate in the greater estate of the nation, relinquished the smaller privilege to be colonists, and gained the greater power to be Americans. They had learned the lesson that to submit is to govern, to serve is to rule.

"Historically considered, this conflict has never ceased. The right of a smaller freedom was the theme of nullification. It was the principle of secession. It is the foundation of all appeals to resist authority, to overthrow government, and destroy property. It is not service, it is not duty, it is not progress. It is the essence of selfishness, the substance of reaction. Against all these forces America has set her face for three centuries."

In that quotation we may find the germ of his effective position at the time of the Boston police strike.

If Mr. Coolidge has a regard for the significance of America's past, he has a live sense of the nation's problems now and for the future. He sees America as a continuing creation. In another address he again emphasizes the need for effort as shown by the past and as demanded now. He says:

"In the change that has marked all peoples America has not remained unchanged. Politically we appear to be the same. Our political institutions, resting on the firm foundation of the people, have not been shaken. They have been assailed, will be assailed, both by the unthinking and the vicious. . . . But how be free, how come into the greatest liberty? Not by casting aside of all restraint, but by the observance of all law; not by lack of self-control, but by an intense discipline; and finally never by ignorance but ever by a larger knowledge of the truth. There may be an involuntary servitude but never an involuntary liberty. It is ever purchased with a great price. It is not given or bestowed, it is acquired. The American people in their sovereignty must forever remember that to set free a king ever requires the ransom of a king."

That Mr. Coolidge's conception of law always takes cognizance of it as something universal and moral, not merely as something legislative, is demonstrated in his talk October 21, 1923, before the Governors' Council in Washington, when he said:

"The law represents the voice of the people. Behind it, and supporting it, is a divine sanction. Enforcement of the law, and obedience to the law, by the very nature of our institutions, are not matters of the choice in this republic, but the expression of a moral requirement of living in accordance with the truth. They are clothed with a spiritual significance, in which is revealed the life or the death of the American ideal of self-government." This recognition of the necessary association between law and liberty is set forth in a letter addressed to the editor of *Scribner's Magazine*, thanking him for an advanced copy of Colonel Roosevelt's letters on labor matters. In his letter Mr. Coolidge said :

"The matter of public order is so clear and so fundamental that it is difficult to see how any one would think of compromising or avoiding that issue. These letters express clearly and concisely the fundamental principles of the relation of the government to labor and industry, and the necessity for an impartial execution of the laws against every force gathered for an

illegal purpose, whether it be in the name of
the employer or the employee. They indicate
clearly that not the private will but the public will must be maintained as the supreme
authority."

Much of Mr. Coolidge's philosophy of government is summed up in the address which
he made before the State Senate of Massachusetts January 7, 1914, on being elected
its president:

"Men do not make laws. They do but discover them. Laws must be justified by something more than the will of the majority. They
must rest on the eternal foundation of righteousness. That state is most fortunate in its form
of government which has the aptest instruments for the discovery of laws. The latest,
most modern, and nearest perfect system that
statesmanship has devised is representative
government. Its weakness is the weakness of
us imperfect human beings who administer it.
Its strength is that even such administration
secures to the people more blessings than any
other system ever produced. No nation has

discarded it and retained liberty. Representative government must be preserved."

Mr. Coolidge respects law as do the American people, seeing in it the only sure guaranty of liberty.

CHAPTER V

OBEDIENCE AND DEMOCRACY

Mr. Coolidge's respect for law as the only sure guaranty of liberty is complemented by his keen realization of the fact that obedience to law is an essential of democracy. His knowledge of history, our own and other nations', has taught him that unless there exists a close and intelligent coöperation between law and those who live under it, there can be no sure continuity of the institutions for free government. It is one of the elements of Mr. Coolidge's statesmanship, and one which he frequently expresses in words, that those who live under the protection and benefits of a law-ordered government owe an inescapable obligation to abide by and obey those laws which exist for them. We find throughout Mr. Coolidge's speeches and writings a reiteration of his faith in the people and of his insistence upon the fact that only by reliance upon the spirit of the public can we have that national coöperation which creates permanence. In one of his speeches he said : "It is time to supplement the appeal to law, which is limited, with an appeal to the spirit of the people, which is unlimited. Such unsettlements disturb, but they are temporary. Some factious elements exist, but they are small. No assessment of the material conditions of Americans can warrant anything but the highest courage and the deepest faith. No reliance upon the national character has ever been betrayed. No survey which goes below the surface can fail to discover a solid and substantial foundation for satisfaction. But our countrymen must remember that they have, and can have, no dependence save themselves. Our institutions are their institutions. Our government is their government. Our laws are their laws. It is for them to enforce, support, and obey. If in this they fail, there are none who can succeed. The sanctity of duly constituted tribunals must be maintained. Undivided allegiance to public authority must be required. With a citizenship which voluntarily establishes and defends these, the cause of America is secure. Without that, all else is of little avail."

This identity of the government with the people, this thought that as the government belongs to the people so also the people are under an obligation to the conscious factors in determining the spirit of the government, is emphasized frequently by Mr. Coolidge. That obedience is a necessary item of sovereignty he not only believes but continually asserts.

Mr. Coolidge's vision of representative democracy is positive and constructive. He does not regard it simply as a departure from, or as a negation of, some other form of government. To him, democracy is an assertion. It is not a tearing-down of despotism so much as it is a building-up of a more potent authority. He recognizes as an omnipresent characteristic of the human race in all times a demand for rulers, a demand for authority, a demand for law. He sees representative democracy to be the most potent, the most just, and the most satisfactory of all conceivable applications of these truths. On these points he touched in an address August 2, 1922, before the Ninth Annual Industrial Conference at Babson Institute, Wellesley Hills, Massachusetts. In this address he said:

"We need a fuller realization and a broader comprehension of the meaning both of political and economic democracy . . . The word democracy is used very inaccurately. . . . The easy way to understand what may be expected of it is first to understand what it is.

"There has never been any organized society without rulers. The great power of mankind has been created through unity of action. This has meant the adoption of a common standard. In most ancient times this was represented in the chieftain. In modern times it is represented by a code of laws. The important factor to remember is that it has always required obedience. Democracy is obedience to the rule of the people.

"The failure to appreciate this double function of the citizen has led to much misunderstanding, for it is very plain to see that there cannot be any rule of the people without a people to be ruled. The difference between despotism and democracy is not a difference in the requirement of obedience, it is a difference in rulers. He becomes an absolute sovereign by absolute obedience. He will be a limited sovereign if he limits his obedience. The criminal loses all his freedom. It is easy to see that democracy will have attained perfection when laws are made wholly wise and obedience is made wholly complete. One of the great tragedies of American institutions is the experience of those who come here expecting to be able to rule without rendering obedience. They have entirely misconceived the meaning of democracy. But they need not disturb its defenders. To cast it aside could only mean the acceptance of a type of rule which had already been discarded. The true hope of progress lies only in perfecting it. Already it is better than anything else in the world. But it rests entirely on the people. It depends on their ability both to rule and to obey. It is

what they are.   The government is what they
make it."

One of the most interesting characteristics
of Mr. Coolidge's ideals and beliefs as they are
displayed by his own words is that he invariably unites a serious comprehension of present
and future problems with a firm faith in the ultimate righteousness of public thought.   He frequently calls upon the people to do their duty,
to obey the law, and to take citizenship seriously;
but he does so with no note of pessimism or discouragement.   He looks forward to a continuing perfection of self-government.   He looks
forward to a steady growth of public understanding.   He builds upon the firm foundation of essential human sanity.   All this we find expressed
by himself in his own speeches.   A man who
never puts forward his own ego, a man who does
not discuss himself, a man who is a stranger to
introspection, he yet reveals himself by his own
words as few statesmen have done.   He does
not assert opinions.   He states basic political
and economic facts.   He has the cold precision
of instinctive exactitude.

CHAPTER VI

THE COMMON CAUSE

Through all of Mr. Coolidge's discussions of
the principles of government there is discernible
a quick appreciation of what may be called the
American community of interests. He has a
lively sense of the common cause in which we
all, as Americans, are enlisted. It is an important item in his mental makeup. "Do not
hesitate to be as revolutionary as science. Do
not hesitate to be as reactionary as the multiplication table." That is what he said in his
address to the State Senate on being elected
its president. It is a gauge of his character.
We find constantly repeated in his utterances
an expression of his conviction that an injustice
to any is an injury to all. In one of his speeches
he reminds us that "an American ideal is equality." He proceeds to define what he understands this to mean: "Not that all are equal

in degree, — there are differing glories, as of sun, and moon and stars, — but all are equal in kind, tolerating no class distinction, no privilege, save that which comes from service; no plutocrat, no proletariat, no authority, save that which is derived from the consent of the people."

Phrasing in another way his emphasis upon equality of potentiality, he said in an address before the Women's Roosevelt Memorial Association at New York on January 23, 1921: "Men build monuments above the graves of their heroes to mark the end of a great life, but women seek out the birthplace and build their shrine, not where a great life had its ending but where it had its beginning, seeking with a truer instinct the common source of things not in that which is gone forever but in that which they know will again be manifest."

Carrying the idea further, and applying it in the field of the achievements of men, he said in the same address: "The sovereignty of the people means the sovereignty not of a self-selected few. It means the supremacy of the matured convictions of all the people. Our franchise is not granted to class or caste. It is the acquired right of all Americans." In those words he expresses his understanding of the universality of the franchise; by inference we find in them also his understanding of the fact of the common cause which enlists all Americans, uniting them both in benefits and in responsibilities. His thought may be fairly assumed to be that not only is the franchise "the acquired right of all Americans," but so also is the obligation to serve this state. Mr. Coolidge sees also the dimensions of the common cause in which the political activities of government and the economic activities of business are inevitably mutually bound. In his address of July 4, 1916, at the home of Daniel Webster in Marshfield, Massachusetts, he made reference to this point, saying:

"Democracy not only ennobled man; it has ennobled industry. In political affairs the vote of the humblest has long counted for as much as the vote of the most exalted. We are working towards the day when, in our industrial life, equal honor shall fall to equal endeavor, whether it be exhibited in the office or in the shop."

Always we find in his speeches the hopeful suggestion of a bettered future. This faith in the future deserves emphasis, because it is in no sense the expression of a man dissatisfied with the present. There are men and women in the world who look forward with a yearning desire for better things, spurred to do so by discontent and by a pessimistic disregard of blessings at hand. It is worth while to differentiate between that kind of forward look and the kind of forward look which characterizes Mr. Coolidge.

Mr. Coolidge's faith in the future starts from the firm foundation of faith in the essential decency of human nature always. "The heart of the American people is sound," he once said. He is cognizant of present ills but sees them as abnormal manifestations and in no sense of being either typical or symptomatic of any organic ailment. All of Mr. Coolidge's philosophy regarding the human race and its potentialities is employed to serve his conception of politics and government. Possessing an essentially philosophic understanding of humanity, he does not indulge it for its own sake, but utilizes it as a guide and sometimes as a definition of the affairs which fall particularly within his province — that is, government. In a much quoted talk on the "Nature of Politics" he said :

"The men who founded our government had fought and thought mightily on the relationship of man to his government. Our institutions would go for a time under the momentum they gave. But we should be deluded if we supposed they can be maintained without more of the same stern sacrifice offered in perpetuity. Government is not an edifice that the founders turn over to posterity all completed. It is an institution, like a university which fails unless the process of education continues."

We are all dedicated to this common cause of maintaining our institutions. Mr. Coolidge in the above paragraph uses the simile of a university, "which fails unless the process of education continues." Certainly this simile is apposite. There is a potent sense of the common cause among college and university graduates. Not only does the process of education continue but other factors in school and college coöperation, characteristic not only of the higher institutions of learning but also of high schools and academies, all operate to maintain traditions and carry forward established purposes.

Quite specific is Mr. Coolidge's emphasis on the common cause of all Americans in his speech on being elected president of the Massachusetts State Senate, from which we have already quoted. At the very beginning of that speech he said:

"This Commonwealth is one. We are all members of one body. The welfare of the weakest and the welfare of the most powerful are inseparably bound together. Industry cannot flourish if labor languish. Transportation cannot prosper if manufactures decline. The general welfare cannot be provided for in any one act, but it is well to remember that the benefit of one is the benefit of all, and the neglect of one is the neglect of all."

That quotation is one wisely to be kept in mind by all who wish to understand Mr. Coolidge, and who wish to forecast his probable attitude toward problems which must come before him.

We have already in another chapter set forth Mr. Coolidge's insistence upon the authority of law. We may here consider the enlistment of that authority as a protector of the common cause. This thought is admirably set forth by Mr. Coolidge in his Memorial Day address at Arlington in 1924:

"When each citizen submits himself to the authority of law he does not thereby decrease his independence or freedom, but, rather, increases it. By recognizing that he is a part of a larger body which is banded together for a common purpose he becomes more than an individual — he rises to a new dignity of citizenship. Instead of finding himself restricted and confined by rendering obedience to public law, he finds himself protected and defended and in the exercise of increased and increasing rights.

"It is true that as civilization becomes more complex it is necessary to surrender more and more of the freedom of action and live more

and more according to the rules of public regulation, but it is also true that the rewards and
privileges which come to a member of organized
society increase in a still greater proportion. . . .

"We need a more definite realization that
all of our country must stand or fall together,
and that it is the duty of the government to
promote the welfare of each part, and the duty
of the citizen to remember that he must be first
of all an American."

This sane reasoning is characteristic of Mr.
Coolidge. He has an accurate sense both of the
binding power of authority in America and of its
helpful force in promoting the cause of all the
people by conferring upon each individual those
protections which are possible only in organized
society honestly and wisely carried forward.

It cannot be too frequently repeated, if we
are accurately to understand this man, that in
championing the common cause of government
and people he neither exalts the state at the
cost of the individual nor supports the individual
in slothful disregard of political responsibilities.
He constantly refers to the imperative duty

of the state to serve the individual; he constantly indicates the equally imperative duty of the individual to serve the state. In an address to the Associated Press on April 22, 1924, he said:

"The principle of service is not to be confounded with a weak and impractical sentimentalism. It does not mean that either the individual or the nation is to assume the burdens which ought to be borne by others. It is warranted in considering self to the extent of recognizing that it is justifiable to accumulate and hold the resources which must necessarily be used to serve ourselves, our own household and our own nation. But it does not stop there. It recognizes also the necessity of serving others, and, when the need arises for meeting a moral requirement, of making individual and national sacrifices sufficient to maintain the cause of righteousness."

From another angle Mr. Coolidge approached the same theme in a speech in February, 1924, while discussing the specific problem of aid to agriculture. He said:

"Very likely you are wondering why agriculture should be discussed here in this metropolis. One reason is that I want to emphasize as forcibly as possible your very intimate dependence upon agricultural welfare. That great interest cannot be affected without the necessity of your being affected. The farm is one of the chief markets for the industries of the nation. You have a direct economic and financial interest. You cannot long prosper with that great population and great area in distress. You have a political interest. The people of those numerous states cast an enormous influence upon the making of the laws by which you are governed. Unsound economic conditions are not conducive to sound legislation. The farm has a social value which cannot be over-estimated. It is the natural home of liberty and the support of courage and character. In all the nation it is the chief abiding place of the spirit of independence."

Mr. Coolidge sees the title of his country in its entirety. He has a reverence for the United States. He holds the state in high regard. He holds states to be sovereign. He binds them all and he binds all within them by his comprehension of the fact that state by state, citizen by citizen, all in all, they are in fact as in title — United. Our country is the United States. Mr. Coolidge carries this political philosophy in all his works.

CHAPTER VII

THE RIGHTS OF THE PEOPLE

Throughout Mr. Coolidge's writings and speeches we find maintained a careful balance in which he weighs both the rights of the people — that is, what the people may properly expect from government and what they can claim by incontestable title — and the responsibilities of the people; that is, what the people must do to sustain and continue those orderly processes without which the social, political, and economic state cannot endure. He sees the state as the expression of human effort in which there is a constant interchange of individual and mass activity. For the protection of the rights of the people he constantly summons the beneficent authority of the state; and for the preservation of such authority he as constantly enlists the conscience and the virility of the people.

This mutual responsibility of state and people,

74

one might almost say this identity of state and the people, binds together his many allusions to the permanence of our institutions. When he emphasizes rights of the individual under government, he implies by his phraseology always the companion and complementary thought of the obligation of the individual to the mass. Thus, in a proclamation for the observance of National Education Week, September 30, 1923, he makes the statement of the obvious that "every American citizen is entitled to a liberal education." But he immediately adds: "Without this, there is no guarantee of the permanence of free institutions, no hope of perpetuating self-government. Despotism finds its chief support in ignorance. Knowledge and freedom go hand in hand." It will be noted that at the same time he stresses the right of the citizen to a liberal education he points out that the utilization of this right carries with it a guarantee for the perpetuation of that very form of government under which the right exists, and by which it is guaranteed. In this same proclamation he says:

"From its earliest beginnings America has been devoted to the cause of education. This country was founded on the ideal of ministering to the individual. It was realized that this must be done by the institutions of religion and government. In order that there might be a properly educated clergy and well-trained civil magistrates, one of the first thoughts of the early settlers was to provide for a college of liberal culture, while for the general diffusion of knowledge primary schools were established. This course was taken as the necessary requirement of enlightened society."

It will be found frequently emphasized in Mr. Coolidge's utterances that he carries forward into the treatment of present problems the essential principles which lie at the bottom of the very foundation of the American nation. This characteristic thought of the man stands forth in the quotation above. While he places emphasis on the right of the individual to education, and while he recalls from history the fact that our country was founded "on the ideal of ministering to the individual," he does not

omit to recall also that provision for colleges
and for primary schools was made in order to
strengthen the educated clergy and civil magistrates. In other words, he sees that from the
earliest beginning of our American civilization
the right of the individual must always, through
its exercise, contribute toward the strengthening of the state, in order that this, in turn, may
the more effectively continue those guarantees
of individual freedom which are the chief characteristics and the highest treasures of American
democracy.

In an address before the Daughters of the
American Revolution he particularly emphasized the need for caution against an excessive
state mechanism, by which the individual might
be smothered and we might erect a dangerous
kind of governing efficiency in which the rights
of the people might disappear. He phrased
the thought thus: "We must not permit the
mechanism of government, the multiplicity
of constitutional and statutory provisions, to
become so complex as to get beyond control
by an aroused and informed electorate. . . .

Good citizenship is neither intricate nor involved. It is simple and direct. It is everyday common sense and justice."

In those sentences he brings forward a thought which may be found with frequency in his writings; which is, that governments exist to serve the people and that they derive their authority from the public will; also, that this proper relation between government and people can be preserved only by "an aroused and informed electorate." Another thought set forth in those sentences is Mr. Coolidge's accurate comprehension of citizenship as a matter which is simple common sense. In an era of almost excessive discussion of problems of government, Mr. Coolidge at all times sees government and citizenship as essentially simple, plain, everyday matters within the comprehension of any normal person. It is on this simplicity of government that he relies for the assurance that the rights of the people can always be maintained so long as the individual keeps his interest alive and his understanding clear.

Once again we find Mr. Coolidge accenting

the balance between government as an institution and the people as its inspiration and support. In an address delivered before the American Bar Association, August 10, 1922, at San Francisco, he says: "Progress has been made by the people relieving themselves of the unwarranted and unnecessary impositions of government. There exists, and must always exist, the righteous authority of the state. That is the sole source of the liberty of the individual, but it does not mean an inquisitive and officious intermeddling by attempted government action in all the affairs of the people. There is no justification for public interference with purely private concerns."

There is a sharp differentiation between Mr. Coolidge's regard for the state and that conception of the state which has existed in some of the old-world countries. While he recognizes and frequently refers to "the righteous authority of the state," he couples with such reference the significant thought that this authority is "the sole source of the liberty of the individual." That is, the reason the state

possesses a righteous authority is simply that
by it the state operates to preserve individual
liberty. If the state ceases to protect such
liberty, if its mechanism becomes so complex
that it loses contact with the comprehension
of the individual, then its authority declines,
and the popular support of it vanishes. We
may gather from his words that he does not
recognize any right of the state to operate
counter to a reasonable independence of action
on the people's part. He has a jealous regard
for the right of the individual to manage his
own affairs and to be left free to his own devices in so far as in doing so he does not run
counter to these functions of the state by which
the liberties of other individuals are made
secure.

The dignity of the individual is a favorite
theme with Mr. Coolidge. We do not find
among his writings long theses on this subject, but we do find throughout them frequent
allusions to it. Single sentences or short paragraphs stand out conspicuously in many places
for the reader who is determined to trace Mr.

Coolidge's thought on the individual man or woman. It was consideration of sharply personal rights which moved him to say, in his address to the Massachusetts State Senate, on being elected its president, January 7, 1914: "Man is born into the universe with a personality that is his own. He has a right that is founded upon the constitution of the universe to have property that is his own. Ultimately, property rights and personal rights are the same thing." Here is a clear understanding of the basic theory of property rights. He declines to be misled into those dim regions wherein are born arguments seeking to identify property rights as somehow oppressive of the individual. He sees with the clarity of those who have read the history of the human race that the right to have property is founded upon something more ancient and something even more substantial than the most admirably contrived governments. He sees that this right "is founded upon the constitution of the universe." He sees that the determination to exercise this right is an essential ingredient of original human nature.   Rights such as these, tracing back even to the origin of the race, no government can successfully undertake to override. By such clear thinking as this, Mr. Coolidge links his political courses of this day with that political philosophy which is fundamental in its authority.

In his first message to Congress, December 6, 1923, he once more stresses the inevitable debt which all organized effort of whatever kind owes to the individual.   This is an illuminating paragraph from that message :

"Our enormous material wealth, our institutions, our whole form of society, cannot be considered fully successful until their benefits reach the merit of every individual. This is not a suggestion that the government should, or could, assume for the people the inevitable burdens of existence. There is no method by which we can either be relieved of the results of our own folly or be guaranteed a successful life. There is an inescapable personal responsibility for the development of character, of industry, of thrift, and of self-control. These do not come from

the government, but from the people themselves.
But the government can and should always be
expressive of steadfast determination, always
vigilant, to maintain conditions under which
these virtues are most likely to develop and
secure recognition and reward. This is the
American policy."

It will not escape the reader's attention that
here again he yokes together the rights of the
people and their responsibilities. He proceeds
immediately from the thought that all we have
built up must, to be successful, benefit the individual, to the thought that in the final analysis every individual must survive and prosper
by his own efforts, the function of government
being not to substitute itself for individuality,
but to remove obstacles from the path of individual development. He sees, and he here
expresses his vision, that as the people deserve
liberty so must they themselves preserve it.
This he truly says is the American policy.

In a talk before the Evanston Sunday Afternoon Club, January 21, 1923, at Evanston,
Illinois, he makes a plea for that toleration by

which the liberty of each one pays due regard to the liberty of the other. "We need to learn and exemplify the principle of toleration," he says. And he continues: "We are a nation of many races and of many beliefs. The freedom of the human mind does not mean the mere privilege of agreeing with others, it means the right of individual judgment. This right our government undertakes to guarantee to all without regard and without punishment to any for following the dictates of their own consciences. It is on this principle that speech is free, the press is free, and religion is free.

"But it must be remembered that there are standards of morality, customs of intercourse, and the laws made in accordance with the public will of the people which must be observed if such freedom is to be enjoyed. It ought to be plain enough that what is wrong for the individual to do, it is wrong, by word or writing, for him to advise others to do. There can be no basis for society on the theory that a person may claim the protection of the laws and yet refuse all obedience to the laws. That would not be toleration but anarchy. This situation always yields to the application of the Golden Rule. We should treat with reverence and respect those things which we hold sacred. We need have no fear but that out of such conduct the truth will prevail."

The rights of the people depend upon responsibility; and by recognition of responsibility these rights are preserved.

CHAPTER VIII

The People's Responsibility

The responsibility of the people for the maintenance of their own liberties is a favorite theme of Mr. Coolidge. He never presents it, however, from the point of view of one who has any fear that the people will be either disinclined or unable to meet all emergencies. He has a firm faith in America and in the people who constitute it. He recognizes the fallibility of human nature, but such is his faith in that form of government under which this nation has grown and prospered, that he believes, and constantly expresses his belief, that under this form the people are more alive to their responsibilities and less likely to commit disastrous blunders than under any other form of government. Throughout Mr. Coolidge's writings we find frequent expression of what may be called the circle of representative democracy — that is, the process by which, under our form of government, the people are best served, and in so being served they contribute most to the strength of the government which is theirs.

In his address, already quoted, before the Evanston Sunday Afternoon Club, January 21, 1923, at Evanston, Illinois, he expresses that thought and says: "It would be folly to argue that the people cannot make political mistakes. They can and do make grave mistakes. They know it; they pay the penalty. But compared with the mistakes which have been made by every kind of autocracy they are unimportant. . . . We have come to our present high estate through toil and suffering and sacrifice. That which was required to produce the present standards of society will ever be required for their maintenance. Unless there is an eternal readiness to respond with the same faith, the same courage, and the same devotion in the defense of our institutions which were exhibited in their establishment, we shall be dispossessed, and others of a sterner fiber will seize on our inheritance. But this is to say that in the teachings of history and in the divine nature of mankind there is every warrant for the profoundest belief that faith and hope are justified and that righteousness will prevail."

Mr. Coolidge sees the performance of responsibilities guaranteed in American character, but he sees also the necessity for frequently reminding the people that successful democracy depends upon their recognition of the fact that they are themselves always and inevitably the controlling factor. He takes frequent occasion to remind us that we cannot evade the burdens of self-government, and that through such evasion, if it occurs, must enter disintegrating forces. In many of his speeches he warns the American people not to expect that from government which government cannot give. He warns against the fallacy that government, as some miraculous institution, can do for the people what they alone can do. Thus in his address of April 13, 1923, at Albany, before the New York State Convention of the Young Men's Christian Association, he points out that "one of the chief errors of the present day is that of relying too much on the government, and too little on our own efforts and on the people themselves." How easy it is for all of us to slip into this slothful way of thinking, or of neglecting to think, all thoughtful Americans know. Earnest-minded statesmen are constantly reminded of it and are continuously in dread of it. Mr. Coolidge himself recognizes the ease with which the people, disinclined to bother themselves with the details of democracy, fall into this dangerous frame of mind. In the Albany address just quoted he says:

"This comes to pass by supposing that, when there is something which ought to be done, we can avoid all personal responsibility by a simple ordinance requiring that hereafter it shall be done by the government. We cannot divest ourselves of our burdens and responsibilities by any such easy method. Where the people themselves are the government, it needs no argument to demonstrate that what the people cannot do their government cannot do. Another error lies in supposing that great fundamental reforms can be at once accomplished by the mere passage of a law. By law is meant a rule of action. Action depends upon intelligence and motive. If either of these be lacking, the action fails and the law fails. These may be stimulated by rewards or penalties, but whatever else may be their effect, they do not remove the source of evil. It is the mind behind the law that makes it truly effective. Laws are insufficient to endow a nation with righteousness."

These are necessary statements of facts familiar to all students of history and government. They are particularly necessary now. We have built up in the states and at Washington a veritable quantity-production series of law factories which grind out laws with a seemingly endless facility, and in response to an apparently insatiable demand. Just as the timid person, instead of correcting his ways of living, rushes at every pain or discomfort to a physician for some powder or potion for relief, so do we incline to hurry to state legislature or to Congress for a formula by which to alleviate economic distress, or to correct some cause of personal discomfort. The temptation to transfer all our burdens to the shoulders of organized government, the temptation to repel our own responsibilities and to "let the government do it," is one of the evils against which all leaders in public life must struggle in behalf of their country. Each legislator or congressman is constantly besieged by a chorus of constituents demanding special legislation, sometimes selfishly inspired, sometimes based on the most patriotic motives; and it is the temptation of these lawmakers to accede to such requests. So the pile of unnecessary bills in state and national legislative bodies accumulates. The vast majority of them fail to become law; but the effort for legislation and more legislation continues. Despite the efforts of wise lawmakers to apply the brakes, the list of laws lengthens. Against this mistaken activity, too often bred in the thought that there is any personal magic in law by which the difficulties of human existence can be set aside, Mr. Coolidge constantly warns.

When he was a member of the Massachusetts State Legislature this peril was constantly emphasized all about him. In his oft-quoted address on being elected president of the State Senate, January 7, 1914, he said: "The people cannot look to legislation generally for success. Industry, thrift, character, are not conferred by act or resolve. Government cannot relieve from toil. It can provide no substitute for the rewards of service. It can, of course, care for the defective and recognize distinguished merit. The normal must care for themselves. Self-government means self-support."

Our government has continued for so long, and has produced such satisfactory results for the American people, that it is easy for us to slip into the insecure but temporarily comfortable position of relying upon the authority, and expecting the automatic operation, of abstract principles of democracy for our salvation. Yet we need no more than a casual reading of our national history to see how perilous such a national frame of mind must be. We need only to recall the days of the declaration of American independence to recognize that those sublime theories, uttered with the authority of the righteousness of human freedom, would have availed little or nothing had not those who framed them in the Declaration achieved their application by courageous and determined action. The Declaration was a magnificent promise. Its results, equally magnificent, were possible only because those who uttered it knew that no statement of theory can suffice without the acceptance of responsibility and a determination to achieve on the part of those who believe in the theory. A foundation is a necessary part of any building. But it is of little importance in the scheme of things unless an adequate structure is built upon it. Our system of representative democracy, our national theories of government, constitute a sure foundation. The structure upon it is never complete. We must forever build. It is the need for continuously wise construction which dictates an alert citizenship and a quick sense of individual responsibility always.

At the dedication of a government hospital for colored veterans of the World War, at

Tuskegee, Alabama, on February 12, 1923, Mr. Coolidge pointed to the fact that theories unsupported, themselves support nothing. In his speech on that occasion he said: "Theories are of very little use in this world which cannot be put into practical operation. The theory of freedom would not help any one unless it worked out by bringing greater happiness and success to those who were in the possession of it. There is very much that the people need which cannot be bestowed upon them by the Constitution, or by laws. If they have it at all, they must provide it for themselves. The government can help, but in the last resort every one must work out his own destiny. Freedom is a high estate. It places on the individual grave duties and grave responsibilities. If these be met and performed, success will follow. If they be neglected and evaded, the end will be failure. To a great extent it is a question of obedience. It was the belief of Abraham Lincoln that all people could and would finally rise to these requirements."

While Mr. Coolidge warns against unreasoning and excessive reliance upon laws for leadership, he does not falter in faith. This faith we must believe is buttressed in his knowledge of the history of his nation. He undoubtedly looks back over the century and a half of our national existence, and he undoubtedly is impressed by the fact that while the seductions of easy government have always beckoned to the indolent, there has been that in the fiber of the American people which has made them always equal to whatever emergencies confronted them, and which in all times of stress, and in all crises, has made them competent and determined to vitalize liberty. In a talk at Wheaton College, Norton, Massachusetts, on June 19, 1923, he sought to turn the attention of his hearers to the need for individual initiative when he said:

"The time appears to have arrived when we may more properly look to the people, when natural laws may well be left to supplement artificial laws. It is necessary always to give a great deal of thought to liberty. There is no substitute for it. Nothing else is quite so effective. Unless it be preserved, there is little else that is worth while. In complete freedom of action the people oftentimes have a more effective remedy than can be supplied by government interference. Individual initiative, in the long run, is a firmer reliance than bureaucratic supervision. When the people work out their own economic and social destiny, they generally reach sound conclusions."

There is nothing mysterious in government. The principles of democracy are essentially simple. It is one of the tasks of statesmen to clarify, rather than to confuse, the truths of government. That government succeeds best and endures longest which maintains the most accurate balance of the rights of the people and their responsibilities. Upon these two factors in the conduct of human affairs all that we as a nation have built up through a century and a half rests. In an oft-quoted paper on the nature of politics, Mr. Coolidge says: "Our institutions are predicated on the rights and the corresponding duties, on the worth, of the individual. It is to him that we must look for

safety. We may need new charters, new con-
stitutions, and new laws at times. We must
always have an alert and interested citizenship.
We have no dependence but the individual.
New charters cannot save us. They may appear to help but the chances are that the beneficial results obtained result from an increased
interest aroused by discussing changes. Laws
do not make reforms, reforms make laws. We
cannot look to government. We must look to
ourselves."

When people rush to legislative bodies for
relief they have little or no thought of the
ultimate consequences of the legislation they
seek. It is easy to ask the government to spend
money; it is easy to forget that the government
has no money to spend, except the people's
money. Mr. Coolidge seeks to keep constantly
before the public mind the thought that in the
last analysis the people themselves pay for what
they get. In an address before the American
Bar Association, on August 10, 1922, at San
Francisco, he touched upon this fact: "When
provision is made for far-reaching action by

public authority, whether it be in the nature of an expenditure of a large sum from the Treasury or the participation in a great moral reform, it all means the imposing of large additional obligations upon the people. In the last resort it is the people who must respond. They are the military power, they are the financial power, they are the moral power of the government. There is and can be no other. When a broad rule of action is laid down by law it is they who must perform. If this conclusion be sound, it becomes necessary to avoid the danger of asking of the people more than they can do."

This portion of his Bar Association speech is of particular pertinence now. There rarely has been a time when so many persons were misled by the thought that in some way the government can do what the people themselves are disinclined to do. The assaults upon the national treasury and upon state treasuries are of a number which jeopardize the public credit. The necessity for economy in government expenditures is acute. The complexity of our modern civilization, the increasing demands for comforts and conveniences lay a heavy burden upon those in authority who would meet these demands so far as reasonable, and who would at the same time prevent the imposition of insupportable loads upon the tax-paying public. The necessity for impressing upon the tax-payer that it is always he who pays the cost of government expenditures is obvious to all leaders in public life. Mr. Coolidge has always had a clear conception of this vital fact of government. Nowhere does he state it more clearly than in this address before the American Bar Association. Continuing on this theme, he says:

"As the standard of civilization rises there is necessity for a larger and larger outlay to maintain the cost of existence. As the activities of government increase, as it extends its field of operations, the initial tax which it requires becomes manifolded many times when it is finally paid by the ultimate consumer. When there is added to this aggravated financial condition an increasing amount of regulation and police control, the burden of it all becomes very great.

"Behind very many of these enlarging activities lies the untenable theory that there is some short cut to perfection. It is conceived that there can be a horizontal elevation of the standards of the nation, immediate and perceptible, by the simple device of new laws. This has never been the case in human experience. Progress is slow and the result of a long and arduous process of self-discipline. It is not conferred upon the people, it comes from the people. In a republic the law reflects rather than makes the standard of conduct and the state of public opinion. Real reform does not begin with a law, it ends with a law. The attempt to dragoon the body when the need is to convince the soul will end only in revolt.

"Under the attempt to perform the impossible there sets in a general disintegration. When legislation fails, those who look upon it as a sovereign remedy simply cry out for more legislation. A sound and wise statesmanship which recognizes and attempts to abide by its limitations will undoubtedly find itself displaced by that type of public official who promises much, talks much, legislates much, expends much, but accomplishes little. The deliberate, sound judgment of the country is likely to find it has been superseded by a popular whim. The independence of the legislator is broken down. The enforcement of the law becomes uncertain. The courts fail in their function of speedy and accurate justice; their judgments are questioned and their independence is threatened. The law, changed and changeable on slight provocation, loses its sanctity and authority. A continuation of this condition opens the road to chaos.

"These dangers must be recognized. These limits must be observed. Having embarked the government upon the enterprise of reform and regulation it must be realized that unaided and alone it can accomplish very little. It is only one element, and that not the most powerful in the promotion of progress. When it goes into this broad field it can furnish to the people only what the people furnish to it. Its measure of success is limited by the measure of their service.

"This is very far from being a conclusion of discouragement. It is very far from being a conclusion that what legislation cannot do for the people they cannot do for themselves. The limit of what can be done by the law is soon reached, but the limit of what can be done by an aroused and vigorous citizenship has never been exhausted. In undertaking to bear these burdens and solve these problems the government needs the continuing indulgence, coöperation, and support of the people. When the public understands that there must be an increased and increasing effort, such effort will be forthcoming. They are not ignorant of the personal equation in the administration of their affairs. When trouble arises in any quarter they do not inquire what sort of a law they have there, but they inquire what sort of a governor and sheriff they have there. They will not long fail to observe that what kind of

government they have depends upon what kind
of citizens they have."

In this chapter we have considered the responsibility of the American people as a whole.
There is another phase of the same problem
which may be differentiated as the responsibility of the individual American. Upon the
subject of individual Americanism Mr. Coolidge has had much to say.

CHAPTER IX

INDIVIDUAL AMERICANISM

If the American citizen needs to have a sense of mass responsibility, he needs to exercise also a lively realization of his responsibilities as an individual citizen. The spirit of our democracy has always been to safeguard jealously individual rights. It has been the theory and practice of our government to interfere as little as possible with the exercise of individual liberty. All efforts to encroach upon this have met with an outspoken and persistent opposition. It follows that the individual, by virtue of his independence, must be worthy of it. It follows also that an individual does not lose his individuality by the circumstance of occupying a public office. A state or national legislator in no respect or degree puts aside his individuality, or evades his duty as an individual American, when he assumes the title and duties of office.

In a memorable veto message, in which Mr. Coolidge, as governor of Massachusetts, on May 6, 1920, vetoed an act known as the Wine and Beer Bill, he said:

"We have had too much legislating by clamor, by tumult, by pressure. Representative government ceases when outside influence of any kind is substituted for the judgment of the representative. This does not mean that the opinion of constituents is to be ignored. It is to be weighed most carefully, for the representative must represent, but his oath provides that it must be 'faithful and impartially according to the best of his abilities and understanding, agreeably to the rules and regulations of the Constitution and laws.' Opinions and instructions do not outmatch the Constitution. Against it they are void. . . . Instructions are not given unless given constitutionally. Instructions are not carried out unless carried out constitutionally. There can be no constitutional instruction to do an unconstitutional act.

"The authority of the law is questioned in these days all too much. The binding obliga-

tion of obedience against personal desire is
denied in many quarters. If these doctrines
prevail, all organized government, all liberty,
all security, are at an end. Force alone will
prevail. Can those intrusted with the gravest
authority set any example save that of the
sternest obedience to law?''

Individual liberty does not mean license at
the expense of other individuals. In our country we have sought not only to achieve and
maintain liberty, but to be worthy of it. All
students of American history know that in our
earliest days the need for an individual realization of the responsibilities of individual liberty
was given weight by the founders of the republic. The details of our government change
to accord with the advance of time and the
adoption of new methods of society; but the
principles upon which our republic rests do not
change. The imperative need for a keen sense
of individual Americanism remains constant.
It is one of the functions, indeed it is one of the
duties, of government to make more certain
the preservation of this national individualism.

Government and laws must strengthen it, not debilitate it. In a talk over the radio from the White House, on February 22, 1924, President Coolidge, in a tribute to George Washington, made some wise observations which are pertinent to the thought here under discussion. The President sees George Washington not simply as a legendary figure about whom have clustered stories of unending variety, but as a clear-thinking statesman who understood the people of his time, and who foresaw the nature of those who would come in later generations. The President understands the vision of George Washington, which was one of faith in the future. Washington set a measure of trust in the individual which has been a continuing characteristic of wise American leadership in all the years since. We find this characteristic exemplified in many of the writings of Mr. Coolidge. We find his acknowledgment of America's debt to Washington in these words of his radio address noted above:

"Washington did not, could not, give anything to his countrymen. His greatness lies in the fact that he was successful in calling them to the performance of a higher duty. He showed them how to have a greater liberty by earning it. All that any society can do, all that any government can do, is to attempt to guarantee to the individual the social, economic, and political rewards of his own effort and industry. The America which Washington founded does not mean we shall have everything done for us, but that we shall have every opportunity to do everything for ourselves. This is liberty, but it is liberty only through the acceptance of responsibility. . . .

"Self-government does not purge us of all our faults, but there are very few students of the affairs of mankind who would deny that the theory upon which our institutions proceed gives the best results that have ever been given to any people. When there is a failure, it is not because the system has failed, but because we have failed. For the purpose of insuring liberty, for enactment of sound legislation, for the administration of even-handed justice, for the faithful execution of the laws, no institutions have ever given greater promise or more worthy performance than those which are represented by the name of Washington.

"We have changed our constitution and laws to meet changing conditions and a better appreciation of the broad requirements of humanity. We have extended and increased the direct power of the voter. But the central idea of self-government remains unchanged. While we realize that freedom and independence of the individual mean increased responsibility for the individual; while we know that the people do and must support the government, and that the government does not and cannot support the people, yet the protection of the individual from the power now represented by organized numbers and consolidated wealth requires many activities on the part of the government which were not needed in the days of Washington. Many laws are necessary for this purpose, both in the name of justice and of humanity. Efforts in this direction are not for the purpose of undermining the independence of the individual, but for the purpose of maintaining for him an equal opportunity. They are made on the theory that each individual is entitled to live his own life in his own way, free from every kind of tyranny and oppression."

Mr. Coolidge has always been cognizant both of the need for individual independence on the part of public officials, and of the difficulties under which they maintain it. In his article on the nature of politics, from which other quotations have been made, he says: "We live under a republican form of government. We need forever to remember that representative government does represent. A careless, indifferent representative is the result of a careless, indifferent electorate. The people who start to elect a man to get what he can for his district will probably find they have elected a man who will get what he can for himself."

Again emphasizing the necessity for individual initiative and for individual utilization of the benefits under a republic, Mr. Coolidge says, in a Memorial Day address at Northampton, Massachusetts, May 30, 1923: "If there be a destiny, it is of no avail for us unless we work with it. The ways of Providence will be of no advantage to us unless we proceed in the same direction. If we perceive a destiny in America, if we believe that Providence has been the guide, our own success, our own salvation, require that we should act and serve in harmony and obedience."

This individual initiative is an essential ingredient of a wise use of the ballot. The growing extension of the franchise in human history brings this individual responsibility into relief. This idea Mr. Coolidge has expressed as follows: "Along with the great expansion of free institutions, which has carried them to all parts of the world in a startlingly brief historic period, there has gone a broadening of the principle of self-government. The ballot in the earlier forms of democracy was the privileged possession of a limited class. . . . But lately we have come upon times in which the vote is esteemed, not as a privilege or a special endowment bestowed only for cause shown, but more in the nature of an inherent right withheld only for cause shown. This new conception makes it no longer a privilege, no longer even a right which may be exercised or omitted as its possessor shall prefer. It becomes an obligation of citizenship, to be exercised with the highest measure of intelligence, thoughtfulness, and consideration for the public concern."

In another address he sounds a note of warning, in which he says that: "The record of past history is the record, not of the success of republics but of their failures. Those now in existence have escaped from overflow time and again by an exceedingly narrow margin." Again we find the note of caution in an address before the National Conference of Mutual Savings Banks, at Boston, on April 23, 1920:

"Our country at the present time is enjoying a greater period of money prosperity than at any other time in its history. That means there is in the hands of the public in general a greater power financially than it has ever exercised in peace. Wherever new powers are acquired by the people, it is always somewhat difficult at the outset for them to take up the corresponding responsibilities. You see that through all the pages of history. You see it especially where a despotic and tyrannical form of government has been overthrown, and the people find themselves for the first time in the exercise of political rights. Their freedom has given them a new power they never had before. I know of no people that has gone through experience of that nature without running into certain excesses. I do not mean by that they should not have had the experience, but I mean that we find in history, where that new power has been given to people in general, it has been used by some with excess."

In a more philosophic vein, at the New York State Convention of the Y.M.C.A. at Albany, April 13, 1923, he still lays stress upon individual responsibility for national success: "Right-thinking people want the results of prosperity, education, and loyalty to the government. The question which is always before us is how these results are to be secured. It is very evident that palliatives fail. The hope of rewards, the fear of punishments, do not go very far. There is very little that is really worth while which can be bought or sold. The desire for gain has made many cowards, but it never made a hero. The country cannot be run on the promise of what it will do for the people. The only motive to which they will continue ready to respond is the opportunity to do something for themselves, to achieve their own greatness, to work out their own destiny.''

By personal conscience human liberties are secured. In the preservation of these all must be enlisted. They constitute the goal of all peoples. At Fall River, Massachusetts, on April 15, 1919, Mr. Coolidge, then governor, said: ''The greatest achievement of government is liberty. Men must put that first. When that goes all that America has gained is lost. It cannot exist without order. Whoever counsels disorder is an enemy of liberty. We have set up the authority of the people. We have processes and methods by which the people put into effect their will; their voice speaks to us from the ordinances of law, from the halls of legislation and of justice.''

CHAPTER X

Coolidge Conservatism

Mr. Coolidge's conservatism is that of one who believes that things worth preserving should be preserved. Like all men whose function it is to build, he faces forward. He has no enthusiasm for change as change alone. He would retain that which has been tested, proved good, and not outworn by the passage of time and alteration of circumstances. He would test new devices and adopt those which qualified. We may suppose that his own philosophy of conservatism is summed up in the oft-quoted words from his speech as president of the Massachusetts State Senate, January 7, 1914: "Don't hesitate to be as revolutionary as science. Don't hesitate to be as reactionary as the multiplication table."

The terms "conservative" and "progressive" are comparative. It is not easy to establish a

precise line of division. Precisions undertake
to create "progressive conservatives" and "conservative progressives"; but this is not very
satisfactory. In these days new ideas and devices are so plentiful in politics that it is hard to
classify any public man and keep him where we
place him. Policies regarded as progressive, or
even radical, in one year fall into the category
of conservative ideas very soon. Presentation of
a new thought in government goes through the
stages of assertion, attack, discussion, debate,
consideration, and may come to adoption. It
then becomes something to be preserved or to be
repealed. Those who are for its preservation
find themselves called conservative, even though
championship of the same thing a few years
back had made them celebrated as progressive.
Our American Revolution was certainly "progressive"; yet it sought to preserve inalienable
rights, and so was an assertion of conservatism.

Mr. Coolidge, as a man active in public life
for a good many years, does not close his eyes
to contemporary movements of thought. He is
clearly aware of the many currents of discontent.

He has a full vision of the forces which industriously seek to substitute things untried for those established. In an address at Fredericksburg, Virginia, July 6, 1922, he said:

"The world to-day is filled with a great impatience. Men are disdainful of the things that are, and are credulously turning toward those who assert that a change of institutions would somehow bring about an era of perfection.

"It is not a change that is needed in our Constitution and laws so much as there is need of living in accordance with them. The most fundamental precept of them all — the right to life, liberty, and the pursuit of happiness — has not yet been brought into universal application. It is not our institutions that have failed, it is our execution of them that has failed.

"The great principles of life do not change; they are permanent and well known. Men are not ignorant of what justice requires. No power can ever be brought into existence which will relieve of obligations. The sole opportunity for progress lies in their faithful discharge.

"There is no reason for Americans to lack confidence in themselves or in their institutions. Let him who doubts them look about him. Let him consider the power of his country, its agriculture, its industry, its commerce, its development of the arts and sciences, its great cities, its enormous wealth, its organized society, and let him remember that all this is the accomplishment of but three centuries. Surely we must conclude that here is a people with a character which is not to be shaken. Imperfections there are, violations of the law there are, but public requirements were never so high in the intercourse of society, in the conduct of commerce, in the observance of the law, and in the faithful discharge of public office as at the present time.

"There are criticisms which are merited, — there always have been and there always will be; but the life of the nation is dependent not on criticism but on construction, not on tearing down but on building up, not on destroying but in preserving. If the American Revolution meant anything, it meant the determination to live under a reign of law. It meant the assertion of the right of the people to adopt their own con-

stitutions, and when so adopted the duty of all
the people to abide by them. The colonists of
that day had had enough of the reign of force.
They had had enough unlawful usurpation of
their government, enough of the domination of
a military force quartered in their midst. They
wanted to escape from the rule of a force imposed from without and live in accordance with
the light of reason which comes from within.
That is the real mark of progress. That is the
true liberation of mankind. . . .

"The industrial life of the nation cannot stand
except on the recognition and observance by
everybody connected with it of the fundamental precepts of American institutions. Nothing
will ever be settled unless it be settled in accordance with them. Any other attempt will have
as its result nothing but confusion, destruction,
anarchy, and failure."

Man is a restless animal. The thing achieved
soon becomes commonplace. He is for new
scenes and new deeds. He is always hasten-
ing onward. It is the spirit of mankind and it
makes civilization. Constructive dissatisfaction

is the force by which the race moves forward.   It
reaches, gropes, and sometimes achieves greatly ;
and sometimes blunders tragically.   Out of a
score of new things tried, one prize is won.
There is to-day a passion for standardization,
for exact limitations, for specifically charted
courses ahead — a feverish insistence upon ex-
actness.   Yet of all things created nothing is
so little standard as the human race.   It halts
and gallops, swims and flounders, climbs and
stumbles, builds and tears down, creates and
destroys, exalts and defiles ; and no man is wise
enough — or foolish enough — to alter this.
Progress?   It is the genius of the race.   The
small boy venturing on his first expedition across
the field after butterflies symbolizes the march of
centuries.   The baby climbing from its crib is
impelled by the same zest for new fields which
has led conquerors around the world and has
opened up the mysteries of dark continents.

Progress is the genius of the race.   Then what,
and who, is the conservative?   He is the man
who, recognizing the inevitable forwardness of
humanity, yet insists upon preserving those

things which best guard against disaster. Such is the honest conservative. The adventurous sometimes call him overcautious. There is an infection in recklessness; yet the reckless might wreck the world were it not for the brakes of a wise conservatism. The world needs the whirling energy of adventure; it no less needs the caution of the thoughtful. Such a conservative, progressing always, we understand Mr. Coolidge to be.

There is another type of conservative. One of that type is for the preservation of all things as they are. He distrusts every new device because it is new. He would change nothing. If that type had forever controlled the world, humanity would still live in caves. There are few of them. Mr. Coolidge is not one.

In much of Mr. Coolidge's writings you find such counsel of caution as this, spoken at Evanston, Illinois, on January 21, 1923:

"If we are not to proceed on the assumption of the innate nobility of mankind, then there must be an assignment of some lower estate. If freedom and equality are not to be maintained, then there must be servitude and class distinction. If all the people are not to be permitted to rule, then there must be a rule of a part of the people. If there is not to be self-government, there must be some form of despotic government. If the individual is not to have the dollar which he himself earns, then he must be forced to hand it over to some one who has not earned it. Those who advocate a change in our standards, a change in our ideals, a change in our institutions, a change in our theory of government, can only proceed in this direction. No other course is open to them.

"The general results of our institutions would appear to be so obvious as to need little defense. If by the increase of civilization we mean the strength and welfare of organized society, the protection and security of the individual, the growth of self-government, the general diffusion of knowledge, a wide distribution of property, the effective direction of productive industry, and the advance of science and invention, there can be no hesitation in declaring that under the system which America represents there has been a most gratifying progress.   This is not to say that in the days of old there were not intellects as keen, nor the perception of truths as profound, as any which characterize the modern mind, but no one can deny that at present there is far greater intelligence and a much wider scope of knowledge.''

Such thoughts as the above are particularly pertinent now.   Many of our institutions are being assailed.   We may, if we choose, grant high motives to those making the assault; but if we see eye to eye with Mr. Coolidge, we may doubt their wisdom.   The conservatism of the President questions the desirability of substituting a system under which America has grown great, and has fostered equality of opportunity, for a different system concerning whose operation we can but speculate.   It is the thought of Mr. Coolidge, we may suppose, that he believes the burden of proof to be upon those who counsel such novelties as require for their adoption the annihilation of established things.   It is the conservatism of a man long in public service, who has watched and weighed.

The essential conservatism of Mr. Coolidge's mind, however, is of older origin than the years of his public service. It is ingrained in him to see that the wisest and most epochal forward movements have had in them the demand for preservation of things worth while. It is by this thought, appearing again and again in his writings, that he unites conservatism and progressiveness. As long ago as his days at Amherst College he evinced this attitude. In 1895, during his senior college year, he won a gold medal offered by the Sons of the American Revolution for the best essay on the causes of the American Revolution. The contest was open to the seniors of all American colleges and universities. In his prize-winning essay Mr. Coolidge has this to say, which is pertinent to present-day consideration of his progressive conservatism :

"Though the injustice of taxation without representation made a good war-cry, it is, in the last analysis, a dangerous principle. But it is easy to grasp, and the common people no doubt fought the war largely on that issue. The fact is, it is a duty to the state to pay taxes, and it is equally a duty to vote. It does not follow that because the state requires one duty it shall require the second.

"But there is another side where the requirement of the state runs over into tyranny. Only on this ground can resistance to taxation be justified. So long as the colonies were a part of the state of Great Britain — and they were so by their charters and by the action of William and Mary — that state had the right to demand not only their property, but their service in the army, and, in the last extremity, their lives. It cannot be, then, that the American Revolution was fought that colonists might escape paying taxes. The great struggle that they passed through must make such a duty seem insignificant. The real principle was not one of the right of the state or the duty of citizens; it was a question of government, a question of form and method.

"It is this that is meant in the statement that the struggle was not between nations, or for new principles. It was not so much a revolution, a propagation of new ideas, as the maintenance of the old forms of representative government, of chartered rights and constitutional liberty. England had fought for this in 1688 and imagined it was secured. But it was so only in name."

That is pretty mature writing for a youngster of less than twenty-three years. He had caught even at that youthful age the conception of stability in essentials which has continued to guide him amid the difficulties of active statesmanship. He saw even then the truth, that our American Revolution was fought to preserve something precious to humanity — that it was not simply a process to destroy a political bond between two nations. He saw how deep the causes went, and he saw how strong the consequences were. Not "a propagation of new ideas" so much as "the maintenance . . . of chartered rights and constitutional liberty." Not a new thing in human thought, that those rights and those liberties had been fought for before. They must always be fought for — not always with guns, but always with courage.

The human race is of so ancient origin that

we can trace it but a little distance back. Behind the earliest records lie centuries for conjecture. The great mystery of the past appears impenetrable. Through countless centuries man has been climbing toward the stars. He must climb for countless centuries more. The history of mankind is an accumulation. All that was, in some sense still is. All that is, in some measure forever will be. All that is to be, will trace its roots back into the dim mysteries of unplumbed antiquity. So it is that in estimating the authority of governments, and in building political structures, and advancing the liberties of the race, there can be no ignoring of the past. Nothing that has been ever is annihilated. Records of human thought and achievement are somewhere permanent. The wise statesman knows that there is some connection between the problems and purposes of present-day undertaking and the history of man's political explorations through the ages. At the annual meeting of the American Classical League, held July 7, 1921, at the University of Pennsylvania, Mr. Coolidge said:

"It is impossible for society to break with its past. It is the product of all which has gone before. We could not cut ourselves off from all influence which existed prior to the Declaration of Independence and expect any success by undertaking to ignore all that happened before that date. The development of society is a gradual accomplishment. Culture is the product of a continuing effort. The education of the race is never accomplished. It must be gone over with each individual, and it must continue from the beginning to the ending of life. Society cannot say it has attained culture and can therefore rest from its labors. All that it can say is that it has learned the method and process by which culture is secured, and go on applying such method and process."

Mr. Coolidge warns of the dangers of ill-considered change. He is for that progress which adds to, but does not destroy. He is for continuing and for guiding the accumulation of society to the end that there may be a net gain discernible in our time. Highly important were his remarks before the American Bar Association, at San Francisco, on August 10, 1922. He spoke as a lawyer in the public service. We have already quoted from that excellent and scholarly address. The portion which we here present bears particularly upon his position as a man facing forward but making sure of each step, and desirous that the nation shall step surely toward safety. From his experience in state and national government he has been impressed not only by the dangers of reckless and undigested legislation, but by the perils of an overemphasis of the authority of government in its contact with the individual. There is a radicalism which seeks to cast aside all restrictions of government; and there is another radicalism, not often so labeled, which seeks to tighten such restrictions. Either implies or impels a sacrifice of customs and procedures with which we have become familiar. Each is an adventure into untested and uncharted ways. Against the perils of both Mr. Coolidge has issued warnings on many occasions. In this Bar Association address, or in that portion of it now to be quoted, he emphasizes the hazards of an increasing centralization of government and an increasing imposition of government fiat upon the individual.   He says :

"The national government has extended the scope of its legislation to include many kinds of regulation, the determination of traffic rates, hours of labor, wages, sumptuary laws, and into the domain of oversight of the public morals.

"This has not been accomplished without what is virtually a change in the form, and actually a change in the process, of our government. The power of legislation has been to a large extent recast, for the old order looked on these increased activities with much concern.   This has proceeded on the theory that it would be for the public benefit to have government to a greater degree the direct action of the people. The outcome of this doctrine has been the adoption of the direct primary, the direct election of the United States senators, the curtailment of the power of the speaker of the House, and a constant agitation for breaking down the authority of decisions of the courts.   This is not the government which was put into form by Washington and Hamilton, and popularized by Jefferson. Some of the stabilizing safeguards which they had provided have been weakened. The representative element has been diminished and the democratic element has been increased; but it is still constitutional government; it still requires time, due deliberation, and the consent of the states to change or modify the fundamental law of the nation.

"Advancing along this same line of centralization, of more and more legislation, of more and more power on the part of the national government, there have been proposals from time to time which would make this field almost unlimited. The authority to make laws is conferred by the very first article and section of the Constitution, but it is not general; it is limited. It is not 'All legislative powers,' but it is 'All legislative powers herein granted shall be vested in a Congress of the United States.' The purpose of that limitation was in part to prevent encroachment on the authority of the states, but more especially to safeguard and protect the liberties of the people. The men of that day proposed to be the custodians of their own freedom. In the tyrannical acts of the British Parliament they had seen enough of a legislative body claiming to be clothed with unlimited powers.

"For the purpose of protecting the people in all their rights, so dearly bought and so solemnly declared, the third article established one Supreme Court and vested it with judicial power over all cases arising under the Constitution. It is that court which has stood as the guardian and protector of our form of government, the guarantee of the perpetuity of the Constitution, and above all the great champion of the freedom and the liberty of the people. No other known tribunal has ever been devised in which the people could put their faith and confidence, to which they could intrust their choicest treasure, with a like assurance that there it would be secure and safe. There is no power, no influence, great enough to sway its judgments. There is no petitioner humble enough to be denied the full protection of its great authority. This court is human, and therefore not infal-

lible; but in the more than one hundred and
thirty years of its existence its decisions which
have not withstood the questioning of criticism
could almost be counted upon one hand. In it
the people have the warrant of stability, of
progress, and of humanity. Wherever there is
a final authority it must be vested in mortal men.
There has not been discovered a more worthy
lodging-place for such authority than the Supreme Court of the United States."

To the mind of Mr. Coolidge a weakening of
the powers of the Supreme Court would not be
progress. He sees American liberties and the
rights of all the people best guaranteed by the
undiluted power of the court. He knows its
history. He is impressed by the record of its
success — which is the country's success. He is
for progress, and he sees progress made possible by the protection which such a court as this
has given and can continue to give.

Mr. Coolidge's thoughts on the American
Revolution have found expression in several of
his public speeches. That it was a war to make
progress certain, that it was not a means for

destruction, he points out in a speech which he made as governor of Massachusetts at the Holy Cross College Commencement in Worcester, Massachusetts, in June, 1920:

"Our nation was founded as the result of a revolution, but we don't want any mistakes made about the application of that term. Those who fought the revolution sought to build up, not to destroy. If we find among us some who point to the revolution as justification of what they advocate, we must look to see if their purposes are to build up and not destroy. Our constituted authority rests on property rights. This civilization is maintained materially by the support of property rights. Without this, the civilization we enjoy would not last. Transportation, industry, and all property would be destroyed. All incentive to progress would cease. The support of our institutions and, aye, of the church itself, would cease if we got away from this principle. It is the public in America that owns the property of America. The time is not far distant when it will be a disgrace for those who are affluent to remain idle, just as to-day it is a disgrace for those who are poor and walk through our streets to refuse to work."

There, indeed, is a sharp rebuke for those who would justify every violent assault upon established institutions by citing the American Revolution and issuing a false draft on history.

If there are any who think that Mr. Coolidge keeps an eye too steadily upon the past, let them consider those words from his address of February 12, 1919, before the Middlesex Club, in Boston:

"It is a great privilege for a party to be able to say that he (Lincoln) was the first President that it elected, but if we are to be anything like what he was, we shall not turn continually to the past; in fact, sometimes it seems that he broke with all the past, and even in that great speech at Cooper Union when he revealed, as a result of careful and painstaking research, what had been the record of those who drew up and through their efforts secured the adoption of the American Constitution, it was not for the purpose of justifying himself and the things that he was arguing for, so much as to show that they had been on the right side. So that if we are to observe that characteristic of his greatness, while we shall look to him with veneration, we shall also look not only to the present but to the future."

Mr. Coolidge has the courage to look to the future. He has also the courage to respect the past.

CHAPTER XI

GOVERNMENT FUNCTIONS

Mr. Coolidge's respect for what may properly be called the American system of government is based upon a long and comprehending study, first of the motives which operated in laying the foundations of this nation, and second of the structure which has been built upon those foundations by succeeding generations for a century and a half. He sees the material success and the spiritual vigor of this republic, and he credits to the system under which our nation has progressed the advances and achievements which have made America great. We find him always on guard against encroachments of one branch of the government upon any other. We find him jealously protecting the rights of the executive, legislative, and judicial branches. We find him on many occasions directing his readers' or hearers' attention to the important part played by the American Constitution in maintaining national strength and in promoting national aspirations. He is suspicious of those easy doctrines which, identifying some specific ill existing under the system as we have known it, counsel a short route to the millennium by cutting down the pillars which for so long have sustained the national structure. We do not find him adverse to changes indicated by growth and experience, but we find him vigorously opposed to changes which involve the destruction of things proved good and not proved outworn.

In an address to the Daughters of the American Revolution, at Washington, he made a typical profession of his faith, saying:

"Here in America we are living under a form of democratic-republican institutions which I profoundly believe to be the best that has yet been thoroughly tested. I say this because our system has gone so far in carefully separating the different departments of the government. In the beginnings of the evolution of government all power was lodged in a single head of the state. The sovereign was at once the legislative authority, the executive power, and the judicial discretion. . . . In the early development of popular institutions the legislative and executive authorities were divided. But not until the founders of our republic had made a further distribution and differentiation of functions was popular government assured. The opportunity to prove its judicial function made the third independent but coördinating factor in the government, and the scheme of a perfected democratic-republicanism was for the first time presented to the world.

"That was the great contribution made by the founding fathers in our Constitution. By virtue of it the people were at last assured equality against the tyranny of any despotic executive and the tyranny of any despotic legislature. Neither of them, nor both of them together, might thereafter impose a lawless will upon a defenseless people. . . .

"Abraham Lincoln said that no man is good enough to govern any other man. To that we might add that no minority is good enough to be trusted with the government of a majority.

And still further, we shall be wise if we maintain also that no majority can be trusted to be wise enough and good enough, at all times, to exercise unlimited control over a minority. We need the restraints of a written constitution."

It will be noted that he emphasizes, as a principal reason for his faith in the American system, the differentiation among the three departments of government. He marks it as a mighty advance that we have so long left behind the day when the sovereign combined in his person all three functions — legislative, executive, and judicial. The development of the legislative and executive branches is of later origin than the assertion of arbitrary power, and by that fact represents the acquired knowledge and the developed wisdom of the race. It was left for America to perfect this allotment of responsibilities. He sees this to have been the great contribution of the founders of this republic. He sees that by this achievement not only was good government made feasible, but the people were in perpetuity protected against future menace from tyranny. The people were provided with permanent defenses. To bind these achievements into an enduring organism upon which future generations might depend, our written constitution was provided.

These are fundamental and perhaps commonplace facts; but in the fever of hysterical political discussion, and in the haste for quick remedies, they are sometimes forgotten by those who know them, or overlooked by the untaught. What Mr. Coolidge keeps constantly in mind is a proper perspective of the functions of government. We find appearing throughout his writings a clear comprehension of the fact that in a republic such as ours, government exists to serve the people. This is a diametrically contrary idea to that of old-world monarchies, in which the people have been regarded as contributors to the desires and needs of the state. In those monarchical nations governments have bothered themselves little about their functions, conceiving them to be simply to serve their own purposes and collect from the public pocket. There the functions of the people, by which they made possible the ease and luxury of a governing class, were matters for consideration. Here we have conceived things differently. We start on the assumption that the people's rights are inalienable, and that the government must perform certain functions to make the guarantee of these rights secure.

It needs to be kept in mind that ours is a representative democracy, and that we proceed under a government of laws and not of men — that the framework of our constitution provides restrictions and checks by which precipitate and ill-considered action is made unlikely. Haste for reform often counsels obliteration of these checks. Thus in pursuit of what may be a good end we imperil the guarantees which have held the government stable through many vicissitudes and difficulties.

The functions of government in our republic do not include an unwarranted and excessive interference with the individual. In a Memorial Day address at Northampton, Massachusetts, on May 30, 1923, Mr. Coolidge says:

"Freedom of action is complete, within moral bounds, under the law which the people themselves have prescribed. The individual is supported in his right to follow his own choice, live his own life, and reap the rewards of his own effort. Justice is administered by impartial courts. It is a maxim of our law that there is no wrong without a remedy. All the power and authority of the whole national government cannot convict the most humble individual of a crime, save on the verdict of an impartial jury composed of twelve of his peers. Opportunity is denied to none, every place is open, and every position yields to the humblest, in accordance with ability and application.

"The chief repository of power is in the legislature, chosen directly by the people at frequent elections. It is this body which is particularly responsive to the public will, and yet, as in the Congress, is representative of the whole nation. It does not perform an executive function. It is not, therefore, charged with the necessity of expedition. It is a legislative body, and is, therefore, charged with the necessity for deliberation. Sometimes this privilege may be abused, for this great power has been given as the main safeguard of liberty, and wherever power is bestowed it may be used unwisely. But whenever a legislative body ceases to deliberate, then it ceases to act with due consideration. That fact in itself is conclusive that it has ceased to be independent, has become subservient to a single directing influence or a small group, either without or within itself, and is no longer representative of the people. Such a condition would not be a rule of the people, but a rule of some unconstitutional power. It is my own observation and belief that the American Congress is the most efficient and effective deliberative body, more untrammeled, more independent, more advised, more representative of the will of the people than any body which legislates for any of the great powers. An independent legislature never deprived the people of their liberty."

Mr. Coolidge's understanding of the legislative functions of the government is based on intimate experience. His service in both branches of the Massachusetts State Legislature, ending with two years as president of the

State Senate, gave him an accurate practical
knowledge of the working of those principles
with which he had familiarized himself in his
study of the history of the Republic.   His legislative record was one of achievement.   He
came to the state legislature from Northampton,
an unknown youth.   He entered that body
without influence, and almost without friends
at the state capital.   He won his way forward
and upward by diligent application to current
problems of legislation.   He became a leader
at the Massachusetts State House while yet in
the legislative branch.   It was his exceptional
sagacity which drew the attention of leaders in
the Republican party of his state, with the
result that the party nominated him for lieutenant-governor.   From that office he was advanced to the governorship, and thence to the
vice-presidency of the United States.   Thus it is
that when he speaks of the legislative functions
in government, he talks from the vantage ground
of a close practical experience.   He is not speaking as a theorist, but as a man who has worked
hard in the laboratories of legislation.   He

knows as a practical statesman that the liberties of the people are secure so long as a nation has a functioning legislative body, quickly responsive to the public will, and accurately representative of the national conscience.

Mr. Coolidge, whenever he considers governmental functions, has in mind the protection and preservation of liberty. He is as concerned with the claims of the few as with those of the many. Something of this thought he brought forth in his inaugural address as vice-president. In that address, referring to the United States Senate, he paid tribute to the dignity of that body in these words:

"To it (the Senate) is intrusted the duty of review, that to negotiations there may be added ratification, and to appointment approval. But its greatest function of all, too little mentioned and too little understood, whether exercised in legislating or reviewing, is the preservation of liberty, — not merely the rights of the majority, they little need protection, but the rights of the minority, from whatever source they may be assailed. The great object for us to seek here,

for the Constitution identifies the vice-presidency with the Senate, is to continue to make
•this chamber, as it was intended by the fathers,
the citadel of liberty."

As he has a deep respect for the American
Congress as a whole, he has a particular regard
for the integrity and the spirit of the United
States Senate.   "Whatever its faults," he says
in his inaugural, "whatever its human imperfections, there is no legislative body in all history
that has used its powers with more wisdom and
discretion, more uniformity for the execution
of the public will, or more in harmony with the
spirit of the authority of the people which has
created it, than the United States Senate."

There will be discovered in these and other
tributes to House and Senate, and to legislative
bodies generally, always the thread of the same
thought, namely, that included in the functions
of legislative operation is always the requirement that existing liberties shall be preserved
and their benefits extended to all citizens.

The President's understanding of the courts
is equally incisive.   There is no vagueness, and

there is no hesitancy, in his attitude toward the functions of the judicial branch of the government.   In his address to the Massachusetts State Senate, January 7, 1914, on being elected its president, he took the opportunity to set forth an important truth sometimes forgotten by politicians:

"Courts are established, not to determine the popularity of a cause, but to adjudicate and enforce rights.   No litigant should be required to submit his case to the hazard and expense of a political campaign.   No judge should be required to seek or receive political rewards."

At a time when the independence of the courts was under assault, Mr. Coolidge's view is heartening to those who believe that the established functions of the judiciary should not be imperiled.

During his service in the presidency, following the death of President Warren G. Harding, Mr. Coolidge has, by his acts, as he had previously by his writings, carefully marked the dividing line between legislative and executive authority.

During the dramatic weeks when the Senate was pursuing its investigations precipitated by the oil-land-lease publicity, this matter of demarkation of boundaries came to the fore as a specific matter. On one occasion, pertinent to these affairs, he said:

"It is not for the President to determine criminal guilt or render judgment in several causes. This is the function of the courts. It is not for him to prejudge. I shall do neither. But when facts are revealed to me that require action for the purpose of insuring the enforcement of either civil or criminal liability, such action will be taken. That is the province of the executive."

A fortnight later, in answer to a request from the Senate that Edward Denby should resign as Secretary of the Navy, Mr. Coolidge again emphasized the prerogatives of office, saying to the Senate:

"The President is responsible to the people for his conduct relative to the retention or dismissal of public officials. I assume that responsibility and the people may be assured that as soon as I can be advised so that I may act with entire justice to all parties concerned and fully protect the public interest, I shall act.

"I do not propose to sacrifice any innocent man for my own welfare, nor do I propose to retain in office any unfit man for my own welfare. I shall try to maintain the functions of the government unimpaired, to act upon the evidence and the law as I find it, and to deal thoroughly and summarily with every kind of wrongdoing."

Mr. Coolidge will never be stampeded.

In the spring of the present year (1924), an acute situation in the Philippine Islands gave the President another occasion for emphasizing the differentiation among the functions of a government such as ours. This he did in a letter to Manuel Roxas, head of the Philippine Independence Mission, opposing in this letter any immediate grant of complete autonomy for the islands. This was in March. The President wrote to Mr. Roxas:

"One who examines the grounds on which is based the protest against the present situation is forced to conclude that there has not been thus far a full realization of the fundamental ideals of democratic republican government. There have been evidences of certain inability, or unwillingness, to recognize that this type of governmental organization rests upon the theory of complete separation of the legislative, executive, and judicial functions."

These several functions of the legislative, executive, and judicial branches must ever serve the people. It is for that they exist, and for nothing else. When he was lieutenant-governor of Massachusetts, Mr. Coolidge, in a presentation speech of a silk guidon given Battery B of Lowell, reminded his hearers: "Of course we look to the past for inspiration, but inspiration is not enough. We must have action. Action can come only from ourselves; society, government, the state, call it what you will, cannot act; our only strength, our only security, lies in the individual. American institutions are builded on that foundation. That is the meaning of self-government, the worth and the responsibility of the individual. In that

America has put all her trust. If that **fail**, democracy fails, freedom is a delusion, and slavery must prevail.''

President Coolidge, firm in his faith in the American people, is insistent that those guarantees which preserve American freedom shall not be jeopardized. He holds sacred those government functions by which a century and a half of liberty under law has been made possible.

CHAPTER XII

Party Government

Calvin Coolidge is a partisan. He believes in political parties. He believes his own party is best. That is why he belongs to it. He knows by study that this country has been built on the foundation of party government. He knows by observation and experience that it can continue to prosper materially, and can preserve the essential liberties of a republic, only by a maintenance of this system. He does not believe that his own party has exclusive possession of all the virtues, or that members of his party are the only honest and able Americans. He does believe that the principles of his party offer better guarantees of success to the nation than the principles of other parties. He does believe that his party, both by its principles and policies and by its leadership and membership, is better equipped to legislate and administer the forms of government

than any other party.   He believes in the existence always of two strong political parties.   He
believes in the desirability of an intelligent and
purposeful opposition.   In short, he believes
that an organized party is the best assurance of
stable government in this republic.   This is the
understanding we receive from his writings.
Whenever he has discussed this subject he has
stressed the need for organization and the need
for a national outlook by all parties.   He repeatedly sounds a warning note against selfish
group government, and against that perversion
of party which disregards minorities, or which
fails honestly to serve majorities.   In an address
to women Mr. Coolidge had this to say of
parties :

"It is necessary to have party organization if
we are to have effective and efficient government.
The only difference between a mob and a trained
army is organization, and the only difference between a disorganized country and one that has
the advantage of a wise and sound government
is fundamentally a question of organization.

"I don't mean by that a narrow and bigoted

partisanship, but one that recognizes the necessity of coöperation one with another, if we are in any way to secure the result that we desire. That has been the model of our country from the time when it was established down to the present day."

Mr. Coolidge's conception of political parties, and his understanding of the nation's need of them, is of great importance now, because he is President and because there is prevalent in many parts of the country a disposition to break down party authority and to disregard party discipline, with the inevitable consequence that party responsibility is diminished. If parties as organizations cannot be called to account for legislation enacted under the assertion of party policies, then we are headed towards a condition wherein political parties will cease to have meaning in the minds of the public. Many circumstances are now contributing towards the disintegration of all parties. How to avoid disastrous consequences of this is the task of those who by conviction believe in the party system.

Political parties have always suffered from

troubles within more than by assaults from without.   Speaking on this theme in a portion of his Memorial Day address at Northampton, Massachusetts, on May 30, 1923, Mr. Coolidge says:

"A growing tendency has been observed of late years to think too little of what is really the public interest and too much of what is supposed to be class interest.   The two great political parties of the nation have existed for the purpose, each in accordance with its own principles, of undertaking to serve the interests of the whole nation.   Their members of the Congress are chosen with that great end in view.   Patriotism does not mean a regard for some special section or an attachment for some special interest, and a narrow prejudice against other sections and other interests; it means a love of the whole country.   This does not mean that any section or any interest is to be disproportionately preferred, or disproportionately disregarded, but that the welfare of all is equally to be sought. Agriculture, transportation, manufacturing, and all the other desirable activities, should serve in accordance with their strength and should be

served in accordance with the benefits they con-
fer. A division of the people or their representatives, in accordance with any other principle or
theory, is contrary to the public welfare. An
organization for the purpose of serving some
special interest is perfectly proper and may be
exceedingly helpful, but whenever it undertakes
to serve that interest by disregarding the welfare
of other interests, it becomes harmful alike to
the interest which it proposes to serve and to the
public welfare in general. Under the modern
organization of society there is such a necessary
community of interests that all necessarily experience depression or prosperity together."

Mr. Coolidge sees patriotism served through
party loyalty. He regards allegiance to a party
as a method of demonstrating allegiance to the
nation. In this same address to women he expressed the thought in these words: "I don't
know of any one that has represented the real
ideals of America any better than those of party
loyalty, either on the one side or the other. Men
of the type of Lincoln and Grant, no less than the
type of Cleveland and Wilson, have been loyal

to their party and desired to have party support
and party government for the purpose of giving
an efficient administration. So that whatever
you may do in that direction I believe will be for
the protection of patriotic principles."   In this
same talk he gives to the women before him, who
represented Republican party organization, some
specific advice — some directions of the way by
which they might advance their party welfare in
the interest of the nation :

"You know the principles that you represent,
the principles for which our party stands, and if
they are to be promoted and translated into sound
government, it will be by electing men and women
to office that represent that thought and that
ideal.   So organize and select as good candidates
as you can, and after they are selected, do what
you can to elect them.   By that method I am
certain you will secure the very best results for
yourselves, and the most patriotic results for
this America which we all love."

Like all true statesmen, Mr. Coolidge in prais-
ing parties does so with the thought and belief
that it is through parties that patriotism is most

efficiently served; and that without parties the difficulties of functioning patriotism would be multiplied. This thought of undiluted devotion to the nation we find expressed many times in his words. He touched upon it, for instance, in an address which he made September 11, 1920, at Manchester, New Hampshire, when he was Governor of Massachusetts:

"The welfare we seek is ever the welfare of America, and, if not of America alone, certainly of America first. At times we seek that welfare abroad, seek it necessarily in the service of other peoples, but we must forever seek it at home and seek it in the advantage of all our people.

"It is for the purpose of advancing that welfare that citizens associate themselves in parties. An association which proposes to seek merely the welfare of its own members is not a political party. It is organized selfishness. It may do a great deal of harm, but it will never be a success. Such an organization will begin by despoiling outsiders and end by despoiling each other. The members can never be satisfied with their own portion. True political parties are formed to

serve the public welfare.   It is only on that basis
that there can be satisfaction, a right to exist,
and a prospect of success."

What are the essential foundations for a political party?   In his Manchester address Mr.
Coolidge indicated them to be found "wherever
an organization exists which supports representative government, responsible to the will of the
people publicly expressed, limited by the consent
of the governed as expressed in a constitution,
with judiciary, legislative, and executive, independent, uncontrolled, save by their conscience
and the law."   Illustrating how upon such a
foundation a party may be erected, he continued: "Such a union gathered around Washington.   Such a government was proposed by
Hamilton.   With them John Marshall supported
the adoption of such a constitution.   For the
expounding and defending of that constitution
New Hampshire gave the nation Daniel Webster.
His plea for the Union was the Republican doctrine of his day.   It strengthened the arm of
Lincoln.   It sharpened the sword of Grant.
Approved by the conscience of the nation, it

takes on immortality. The support of these principles is a perpetual foundation for the perpetuation of a great and permanent political party."

This subject of party organization and party government is less discussed than many kindred matters by Mr. Coolidge. His thoughts turn to more comprehensive things. He thinks in national, rather than sectional, terms. He is more interested in American problems than in party problems; the latter interest him chiefly in so far as through their solution he can approach the problems of the country's government. The political party is to him an agency by which objectives of national value are to be sought. He does not look upon the party as a thing apart, as an end in itself, as a final objective. This we gather from his writings. In nearly every instance where he makes allusion to political parties he couples with such allusion some clear emphasis on national needs. Thus, in a speech before the Republican Commercial Travelers' Club, in Boston, on April 10, 1920, he joined partisan and national requirements in these words:

"Parties do not maintain themselves. They are maintained by effort. The government is not self-existent. It is maintained by the effort of those who believe in it. The people of America believe in American institutions, the American form of government, and the American method of transacting business."

In this same speech he renews emphasis on the futility of any party activity which omits the national view. "Any law or rule of action," he says, "which undertakes to set off one part against another is based on a fiction which does not exist and which cannot be carried out, and only leads to disaster." He knows that a political party must have "an abiding faith in the common sense of the American people."

CHAPTER XIII

Matters of Patriotism

Calvin Coolidge asserts and practices a forward-looking patriotism. To him it is nothing static; it is dynamic, purposeful, continuous, and constructive, never bound by limitations of time; it is never the record of a completed achievement. He preaches the doctrine of America first, but always with the necessary corollary that this preference is to be maintained not for self-seeking profits, or the injury of others, but for the preservation of standards, for the promulgation of ideas, and for the accomplishment of purposes in humanity's behalf. If this nation stands for things worth while, it can make those things of value in the world only by preserving a national strength adequate to their dignity and continuance. We have built up here not only a great material prosperity, but a spiritual leadership which has commanded the confidence of other peoples. Our national course has not been one of conquest or exploitation. Patriotism has not for Americans meant restrictions upon the liberties of others, but rather an encouragement to them. Our national influence has been exerted to make independence feasible throughout the world. Mr. Coolidge, as we understand his words, not only has an abiding faith in America, but knows with the assurance of tried statesmanship that only by such faith can the destiny of the nation be made clear in the eyes of the world.

Mr. Coolidge's patriotism is not simply an expression of satisfaction with the past, or contentment in the present. It is a call for enlistment. He summons his fellow-Americans to a unity of service; and he places the preservation of the country's ideals in the hands of the people themselves. In an address to the Associated Press, on April 22, 1924, he thus expresses his thoughts on America's duty to itself:

"Our first duty is to ourselves. American standards must be maintained. American institutions must be preserved. The freedom of the people politically, economically, intellectually, morally, and spiritually, must continue to be advanced. This is not a matter of a day or a year. It may be of generations, it may be of an era. It is for us here and now to keep in the right direction, to remain constant to the right ideals. We need a faith that is broad enough to let the people make their own mistakes. Let them come unto knowledge and understanding by their own experience. Little progress can be made by merely attempting to repress what is evil; our great hope lies in developing what is good. One newspaper is better than many criminal laws. One schoolmaster is better than a legion of bailiffs. One clergyman is better than an army with banners. These are our guarantees of internal peace and progress."

This is a presentation of patriotism in no sense narrow, and in no degree chauvinistic. The inference is in behalf of patriotism as an obligation, not as an indulgence or easy satisfaction. By what as a nation we have done, we gain strength to do more. By serving great causes greatly, and only so, we can serve America. A proper patriotism takes cognizance of the patriotism of others. We cannot love our country more by failing in respect for others. Ideals know no geography. Patriotism takes heed of boundary lines, but its vision sees beyond them. The contacts of the wisely patriotic nation are not conceived in selfishness and prosecuted in hostility, but are bred in thoughts of progress, and are extended by commitment to service. In addressing the American Legion at Kansas City, Missouri, on October 31, 1921, Mr. Coolidge, then vice president, preached the liberal patriotism of a broad-minded statesman when he said:

"Our own national existence presupposes the national existence of others. Were there no other countries there would be no choice between countries, and therefore no loyalty to one to the exclusion of others, no patriotism. That virtue we claim for ourselves we must recognize in others. If it be well for America to have a strong national spirit, it must be well for others to cherish the same sentiment. The war did not break this spirit; in any free country it strengthened it, strengthened it for the glory

of all. America first is not selfishness; it is
the righteous demand for strength to serve.
And America has been dedicated to an unselfish
service. . . . It will not be, then, in diminishing but in enlarging the national spirit that
true progress for the race will be found. There
can be no society without a home, no civilization
without citizenship."

These are the conclusions of a man who
throughout his life has made a study not only of
the facts of history, but of the spiritual authority
of races and nations everywhere. He embodies
in the thoughts quoted the idea that our emotions and sentiments as applied to political
matters of national dimensions are, in a great
measure, limited. We form conclusions by utilizing possibilities of comparison. We assert
basic principles of conduct for individuals and
for races, but in reckoning the fruits of application we have to take heed of what all nations
have done with those principles. In other words,
patriotism embraces something more than a
veneration for abstract theories and doctrines
for conduct. It embraces, and cannot omit to

consider, the practical operation of theories as applied in the development of governments and the stimulation of states to the achievement of material success. In that Memorial Day address at Northampton, May 30, 1923, from which we have already quoted, Mr. Coolidge says:

"Patriotism is easy to understand in America. It means looking out for yourself by looking out for your country. In no other nation on earth does this principle have such complete application. It comes most naturally from the fundamental doctrine of our land that the people are supreme. Lincoln stated the substance of the whole matter in his famous phrase, 'government of the people, by the people, and for the people.' The authority of law here is not something which is imposed upon the people, it is the will of the people themselves. The decision of the court here is not something which is apart from the people; it is the judgment of the people themselves. The right of the ownership of property here is not something withheld from the people; it is the privilege of the people themselves. Their sovereignty is absolute and complete. A

definition of the relationship between the institutions of our government and the American
people entirely justifies the assertion that: 'All
things were made by *them;* and without *them*
was not anything made that was made.'

"It is because the American Government is
the sole creation and possession of the people
that they have always cherished it and defended
it, and always will.   There are two fundamental
motives which inspire human action.   The first
and most important, to which all else is subordinate, is that of righteousness.   There is that in
mankind, stronger than all else, which requires
them to do right.   When that requirement is
satisfied, the next motive is that of gain.
These are the moral motive and the material
motive.   While in some particular instance they
might seem to be antagonistic, yet always, when
broadly considered or applied to society as a
whole, they are in harmony.   American institutions meet the test of these two standards.
They are founded on righteousness, they are
productive of material prosperity.   They com-
pel the loyalty and support of the people be-

cause such action is right and because it is profitable."

Here Mr. Coolidge indicates his very clear conception of the distinction between a representative democracy such as ours and despotisms such as through many centuries characterized the Old World. The ancient selfish doctrine was that material profits must first of all be obtained, and that then it would be a simple matter to justify whatever had been done in obtaining them. That was the old fallacy of going relentlessly forward towards a selfish end, and then presenting, if challenged, an assertion of righteousness corruptly contrived. It lacked even the dignity of the more modern cynical convenience expressed in the phrase that the end justifies the means. Upon that old idea, in which the people have no rights that vested authority is bound to respect, was built the menacing structure of caste and class privilege. It begot a host of evils, but in the end made inevitable the triumph of better things. Like all untruths, it destroyed itself. It was for America, as a new nation, first to set the measure of progress in government. This our country did by sweeping away utterly the old untruth and by determining a righteous course of procedure, confident that the results would not penalize the righteous.

Under the despotic régime there was little patriotism. There was instead a pandering to self, a perversion of good emotion, for the gratification of hateful desires. Subject peoples served despotic authority because they had to, or from the love of adventure, or because thus was opened the only road for safety and potential profit. Despotic rulers maintained the grandeur of their states, not from love of the people, but because through power lay profit. The rule of conduct often was "serve yourself at your country's expense."

Of course there were heroes and there were unselfish men and statesmen in all days. Men were moved by patriotic impulses and were carried ecstatically forward by essentially national convictions. There have been in all eras men of vast vision, self-sacrificing men; but these did not determine the courses of empire nor did they suffice to set up enduring democracy. The flavor of the older forms of government was given usually by those who either themselves sought selfish rewards, or who served such desires in others. In Mr. Coolidge's Memorial Day address just quoted we find expression not only of his personal conception of American patriotism, but also of that spirit which, established at the foundation of the nation, has characterized and controlled its courses since. He says that patriotism in America "means looking out for yourself by looking out for your country." This is the antithesis of selfishness; but by it individuals prosper. By the prosperity of our country all who live here are served. Any act of an individual which is harmful to the country reacts against individual welfare. This is a fact. It is one of the great facts of American history. It is too often overlooked. Mr. Coolidge emphasizes it wisely.

Nor does Mr. Coolidge merely throw out an assertion. This correct reading of American patriotism is justified in Mr. Coolidge's comprehension of the significance of our form of government. "The authority of law here," he says, "is not something which is imposed upon the people; it is the will of the people themselves." In other words, we might say that the only government is the people; that the large army of men in public office, making and administering laws, rendering decisions from the bench, all are there as trustees or as representatives of the public, and for no other reason and with no other power but to carry forward that with which they have been intrusted. It is this identity of government and people which distinguishes our republic. And it is this identity which makes inexorably true Mr. Coolidge's statement that patriotism in this country means the welfare of the individual through the welfare of the nation.

If Mr. Coolidge has faith in his country as expressed in terms of government, he has an equal faith in human nature. Possibly it is the same thing, for our political establishment provides, as no earlier created government ever did, for the operation of human nature in governmental affairs. In the address quoted he notes the two fundamental motives which inspire human action — righteousness and gain. By "gain" he does not mean greed. The man who plants seeds in his garden hopes for gain in the form of vegetables. There is nothing ignoble in seeking for gain, unless by so seeking there is infringement on others' rights. Mr. Coolidge believes that in mankind the strongest element is that which requires him to "do right." To this he regards all else as subordinate. When righteousness is satisfied, and only then, he admits the motive of gain as permissible. Thus he here again emphasizes the difference between our form of government and that of the old despotisms where might alone ruled. Here we place righteousness first; effort for material gain follows satisfaction of the moral motive. Mr. Coolidge observes that "American institutions meet the test of these two standards." They were meant to do so.

This Memorial Day address serves eloquently to elucidate for students an important characteristic of the President. He is neither an impractical idealist nor a materialistic politician. He has ideals; he knows that ideals are of little value to the people unless they can be translated into action and become the guiding factors in processes of government and life. Thus he links a pure idealism with a thoroughly practical understanding of the need and worthiness of material gain. Perhaps it is this unity of thought on these two motives in human nature which has carried him so far and held him so high in the respect and admiration of Americans.

In an address, June 17, 1918, before the Roxbury, Massachusetts, Historical Society, in celebration of the anniversary of the Battle of Bunker Hill, Mr. Coolidge further identifies the relation between those things which occupy a people's thoughts and their moral and mental development. He says:

"What men worship that will they become. The heroes and holidays of a people which fascinate their soul reveal what they hold are the realities of life and mark out a line beyond which they will not retreat, but at which they will stand to overcome or die. They who reverence Bunker Hill will fight there. Your true patriot sees home and hearthstone in the welfare of his country."

It is not without meaning that Americans have
for so long done reverence to national ideals.
Such reverence grows by what it feeds upon.
Revering righteousness, a nation approximates
that which it reveres. We like to believe that in
America we have so accustomed public thought
to worthy national ambitions that the consummation of such ambitions is continuously
feasible. The great figures in American history
all show moral leadership. The utter unselfish-
ness and steadfast courage of George Washington, and the inspired self-abnegation of Abraham
Lincoln, have erected in the minds of Americans
a form of hero-reverence in which these heroes
are not less mighty than the picture of them
which we learn to love. Mr. Coolidge records
his understanding of the accuracy with which the
heroes of his country both reflect and stimulate
the righteous patriotism of his countrymen.

America to President Coolidge is more than
the home of material opportunity. It is more
than a laboratory for the practicing of experi-
ments in abstract righteousness. In many of
his addresses he has emphasized the obligations

which rest upon the shoulders of all citizens, and
he has counseled a rigorous observance of those
laws by which and by which alone American
liberties are made secure.   But beyond all this,
he sees the grandeur of that great structure, the
American nation.   He sees the symbolism of the
Stars and Stripes; for, as he says in a Flag Day
Proclamation of May 26, 1919:

"It was never flaunted for the glory of royalty,
but to be born under it is to be a child of a king,
and to establish a home under it is to be the
founder of a royal house.   Alone of all flags it
expresses the sovereignty of the people which endures when all else passes away.   Speaking with
their voice, it has the sanctity of revelation.   He
who lives under it and is loyal to it is loyal to
truth and justice everywhere.   He who lives
under it and is disloyal to it is a traitor to the
human race everywhere.   What could be saved
if the flag of the American nation were to
perish?"

There is in every land a form of static patriotism which boasts of the past.   Mr. Coolidge's
idea of patriotism is not that.   Venerating the

achievements under the American flag, glorying in its symbolism, he would hold it aloft as a banner to rally the righteousness of a free people in common cause for the protection of liberty and for the inspiration of free men.

CHAPTER XIV

Government and Business

Patriotism is a positive, not a negative, quality. It has been nourished in our country by processes of strength, not of weakness and dependence. Americans have ever been self-reliant. The world has not seen a greater steadfastness of purpose than was manifested by those who first set this nation on its feet. These founders of the republic did not set out to form primarily a government which should be served by the people. Their objective was the welfare of the people in this country, and to serve that they created a government. It was to the people, not to the government itself, that they looked for strength. The American Declaration of Independence was an assertion of initiative by free men. It was not a pronunciamento from an established state. This note of individual self-reliance has characterized the history of our country and has been the continuous motive power for our prosperity. There never has been a time, except in moments of acute emergency, when initiative did not come from the people themselves rather than from any government establishment. It has not been by the fiat of law that we have grown. It has not been by leaning on the government that we have become strong. The ability of the American people to manage their own affairs is the outstanding characteristic of the race.

With these facts of history Mr. Coolidge is of course familiar. He is impressed by them. He is guided by them. By their authority he would guide others. His philosophy is one of strength. He is instinctively distrustful of measures and tendencies which would transfer initiative from the individual to the government. He respects the vigor of American business life. He does not regard profits as necessarily reprehensible. His thoughts do not run parallel to the thoughts of those who consider an honest self-interest to be *per se* inimical to the public interest. He will not allow himself to be misled by sophistries.

At a dinner of the Associated Industries, in Boston, on December 15, 1916, he makes reference to profit:

"We have established here a democracy on the principle that all men are created equal. It is our endeavor to extend equal blessings to all. It can be done approximately if we establish the correct standards. We are coming to see that we are dependent upon commercial and industrial prosperity, not only for the creation of wealth, but for the solving of the great problem of the distribution of wealth. There is just one condition on which men can secure employment and a living, nourishing, profitable wage for whatever they contribute to the enterprise, be it labor or capital, and that condition is that some one make a profit by it."

Nor is Mr. Coolidge attracted by those theories of economics which deprecate the accumulation and use of capital. He believes in capital. He does not believe in it as an indulgence for selfishness; he believes in it as offering the surest guarantees of prosperity for all persons, employer and employed. He sees in

the uses of capital the widest possibilities for
general benefit. He sees in them the only
proven way to develop industrial vigor. He
nowhere warrants the thought that he would ex-
tenuate abuses of or by capital. He frequently
reminds us that he would not penalize a system
which he believes to be on the whole good, because of individual abuses of it. In his mind
capital is one of the evidences of progress. History indicates to him that it was preceded by a
less satisfactory system, or lack of system; and
he warns against policies destructive to capital's
opportunities, expressing the fear that such
policies would turn civilization backward toward an abandoned and discredited economic
past. Such a view of capital he presents in an
address as commencement day orator, June 28,
1920, at the University of Vermont:

"The accumulation and investment of capital
is the means of advance and comfort in modern
civilization, and whatever arrests, discourages,
or prevents it, turns toward distress and barbarism. Whoever the owners, by the nature of
things no power can prevent the capital invested

in business enterprises from inuring to the public benefit. Unless it serves it fails. Capital and brains, investment and enterprise, are not the enemies and masters of the wage-earner, but his friends and servants."

It is suggested by such remarks that Mr. Coolidge would view with hesitation suggestions for government interference or participation in business, unless circumstances indicated an acute necessity. Holding in mind, as he does, the record of industrial achievement in this country based on individual initiative and made possible by the reasonable expectation of profit and the reasonable security of capital, he is loath to see the government place its official hands upon this structure tested by experience. Against the frequent assertion, or suggestion, that capital and investment are oppressive forces, he presents the thought that they are means, and the surest means, by which the wage-earner may himself progress.

There is nothing in Mr. Coolidge's writings to bring comfort to any who, by the abuse of the powers of capital, would exploit the less powerful. There is in his writings no trace of sympathy for the ruthlessness of arrogance in industrialism. He is for the rights of all Americans. He does not omit to consider the rights of those who, having capital, invest it and apply it constructively as well as honestly. His philosophy of the compatibility of righteousness and success, noted in another chapter, influences his thoughts on this subject of capital. Unless capital serves, he says, it fails. Thus he argues — or rather, takes for granted — that the ultimate beneficent results of the capital system are to some extent automatic. In his mind he has summed up the evidence, and he declines to convict capital in its entirety for the offenses of the few. Capital, to him, spells strength. On this line he spoke in his Boston Associated Industries Dinner speech, already quoted in part, as follows:

"We have had many attempts at regulation of industrial activity by law. Some of it has proceeded on the theory that if those who enjoyed material prosperity used it for wrong purposes, such prosperity should be limited or abolished.

That is as sound as it would be to abolish
writing to prevent forgery. We need to keep
forever in mind that guilt is personal; if there is
to be punishment, let it fall on the evil-doer; let
us not condemn the instrument. We need
power. Is the steam engine too strong? Is
electricity too swift? Can any prosperity be
too great? Can any instrument of commerce
or industry ever be too powerful to serve the
public needs?"

During recent years we have seen the government besieged by those who sought from it relief from burdens. Those who wished to restrict
the operations of private investment, and those
who wished to protect it against all risk of loss,
have vied with one another in seeking legislation
which should serve their particular and immediate purposes. Mr. Coolidge has viewed this
tendency with some apprehension, if we may
judge by his speeches over a number of years.
In the paragraph above quoted we find an eluci-
dation of his ideas in the face of such efforts to
obtain government action which should limit
the powers of investment and capital. This

is not the only speech in which he has cautioned against the danger which he believes to lie in plans to hamper that industrial development which has for so long characterized America. He shows clearly enough that he is well-informed concerning wrongful use of material prosperity, but he shows with equal clearness that he does not regard such abuses either as typical or as adequate reason for destroying an entire structure to correct occasional defects. In that speech, as in many others, he places emphasis by inference on the thought that our country is founded upon strength, and that the American people have been able to use strength intelligently and for the welfare of the majority. It may be taken as his idea that if we are to judge nations or political and economic systems solely by their mistakes and flaws, we shall have nothing left but chaos. Identifying essential truths of democracy, Mr. Coolidge declines to allow his mind and judgment to be fogged by false issues.

It was some years ago that Mr. Coolidge wrote his ideas on "The Nature of Politics," from which quotation has already been made in this

volume.   It is one of the most illuminating of
his writings.   Sentences from it are particularly
pertinent to-day and deserve to be kept in mind
during sessions of Congress in the near future.

In it he reiterates his philosophy of strength.
It may be that his upbringing as a farmer's boy
in the rough country of the Vermont hills ingrained in him a respect for work and a recognition of the fact that nothing worth while is to be
obtained in this world without it.   He knew by
experience both the necessity and the dignity of
toil.   When his forbears settled in that Vermont
region, it was practically a wilderness.   They
literally hewed their living from forest and field.
The traditions of his family, the atmosphere of
his upbringing, the history of his state, the visible
achievements in the form of farms and farming
at Plymouth, Vermont, all contributed to anchor
in his youthful mind a clear-minded understanding of the inevitability of hard work.   In con-
trast he saw not only the futility but the menace
in pursuit of ease and evasion of responsibility.
In this paper on politics appear these lines:

"There has of late been held out the hope that

government could by legislation remove from the individual the need of effort. The managers of industries have seemed to think that their difficulties could be removed and prosperity insured by changing the laws. The employee has been led to believe that his condition could be made easy by the same method. When industries can be carried on without any struggle, their results will be worthless, and when wages can be secured without any effort, they will have no purchasing value."

The tendency to run to the government for relief from the consequences of conditions which no act of government caused, and which no device of government can correct, is one of the perils of all states. Statesmen with a knowledge of history have always had to fight against this peril. Men placed in high office have soon discovered the necessity for trying to counteract such a tendency. The significant thing in Mr. Coolidge's character, for those seeking to comprehend his ideals, is that he was fully conscious of this peril to efficient government long before he had reached high executive position. The inclination to draft government aid for extrication from economic difficulties is further complicated, or increased, by those active in politics, who, to gain favor, or because they hold views of government divergent from those which have characterized American history, promise panaceas and offer guarantees of assured prosperity and happiness in the name of that government authority to which they aspire. Some years ago there was a popular slang phrase, "let George do it." A political catch-phrase to-day is "let the government do it." There is little that the government can do beyond protecting the rights of the individual, imposing obstructions against the predatory and corrupt, and facilitating the operation of individual initiative plus hard work. Mr. Coolidge as President now finds himself face to face with a practical test of those ideas which have been his, and which he has preached, for many years. He finds his ideals now to be of pertinent importance.

Much of the reason for the increased swing of public thought towards government help is the natural outgrowth of the abnormal conditions in-

separable from the war years.   Republics do not
break down in time of war; but they find it
necessary to adopt for the emergency some of
the arbitrary devices of despotism.   There has
to be sometimes a more positive assertion of
the authority of the state.   This is done in no
departure from the principles of democracy or
republican government, but, on the contrary, in
an accentuated application of them.   In time of
war a republic, secure in the confidence of the
people, must act by a sort of power of attorney
to represent them and to effect their will by
the shortest and most effective possible means.
When a republic in wartime utilizes some of the
methods of a despotism, it still in no way re-
sembles that arbitrary form of government;
for it is distinguished from it by a sharp differentiation in motives.   The despotism exerts
arbitrary authority of its own will and for its
own purposes.   A republic exerts similar authority by warrant of the people's will, and it
exerts it in behalf of, and for the benefit of,
the people themselves.   Also, under such circumstances of war, there is an implied pledge

to return to normal republican conditions as
soon as the emergency has passed. This the
people under a free government know. In that
knowledge they are secure.

The experience of the United States during the
World War ran true to such a formula. We
found it necessary to do great things expensively,
because it was the conviction of all patriotic
Americans that no price was too high to pay for
that victory without which there could be no
guarantee for the continuing safety of this
nation. During the war we talked and thought
not of cost, but of results. We acquiesced in
methods which by common agreement were held
necessary, wise, and proper then, but which
could not be maintained, or even successfully
initiated, under normal conditions in our land.
Yet there were those who fell under the spell
of government might. There were those who
thought it might be well to carry into times of
peace a greater measure of state authority and
a larger degree of governmental direction of
private affairs than had been hitherto known
here. From this frame of mind, also, came a

new crop of suggestions for governmental interference with industrial and commercial undertakings. Seeing many evils and difficulties about us, there was the temptation to overcome them by short cuts of legislation and by enlistment of an extended bureaucratic government system. Here was a movement, almost entirely well-intentioned, which yet struck at the very roots of American tradition and custom. Of those who most clearly saw this danger, and most clearly warned against it, is Mr. Coolidge. In an address before the Home Market Club, at Boston, on May 14, 1920, when he was Governor of Massachusetts, he made this reference to the subject:

"During the conduct of the war it was necessary for the government to be given and to assume the most arbitrary of powers. We had but one thing in view at that time, and that was the winning of the war, and everything else was sacrificed for that particular object. That is over now. Some of those arbitrary powers are powers people like to use. They like to have prices fixed for them on something they are going to buy, but they would not like it and would not relish it if prices were fixed for things they were going to sell. But what we need to do is to escape as soon as possible from the exercise of arbitrary powers and come back again to the natural economic relationships of supply and demand. We want to get the government out of business. That will mean in its inception, I know, something of abuse, but in the long run it will be more profitable.   It will do more to settle prices, it will do more to relieve us from unrest, it will do more to curb profiteering than any other action it would be possible for us to take."

Mr. Coolidge, if we are to judge by his written and spoken words, desires as little interference with business by the government as possible. Protection of the public against exploitation does not mean, in his political philosophy, a seizure of the avenues for legitimate private profit and their policing by government bureaus or agents.

Applicable to immediate issues is his remark, in the course of an address at the Bates College commencement, June 23, 1920, at Lewiston, Maine:

"There are times when it is necessary to fix prices, times of distress and times of public exigency that require that it shall be done, but, speaking generally, it is a dangerous operation and one that we should pursue only in case of great necessity."

Also applicable at this time is a reference by him, in that same address, to the proposal to ease economic difficulties by a limitation of production. The essential falsity of such a plan is stated concisely in this paragraph:

"There is abroad a disposition to limit production. I think I have said enough to indicate that I do not favor that kind of a proposition. And the fundamental reason is that this world of ours is so made that it is not profitable for a man to be anything but his best. The best that is in us is required of us at all times, and the giving of it will never work to the injury of the public or any of its individuals. We have accomplished a great deal; we are provided with great resources and out of them we shall be able to maintain ourselves."

Mr. Coolidge constantly manifests his faith in the American people. It is rooted in his knowledge of them — a knowledge obtained first by the reading of history, and second by his years of experience in political life. It is upon them that he relies for the continuation of America's material and moral prosperity. He identifies and he pillories the error of supposing that America's strength lies primarily in the functioning of government; he sees that government here derives its authority from the people, and that it is strong only as the people are strong. He resists proposals which, in his judgment, would debilitate the people. He believes that to add strength to the government by transferring it from the people would in the end make government entirely impotent. "The destiny of America," he told the Bates College students, " depends, not upon its resources, and not upon its powers. It depends upon the disposition of the American citizen."

It is upon the foundation of his faith in the

American citizen that he builds his understanding of government.   And it is by the strength of his faith in the people that he conceives the government's best service to them to be one of as little interference with individual initiative as possible.

CHAPTER XV

Economy and Finance

Mr. Coolidge's philosophy of civilization includes utilization of all the fruits of civilization, but demands that these be adapted and applied ultimately for the public's benefit. Throughout his writings he demonstrates a capacity to distinguish between the use and the abuse of all factors in modern life. It is constantly impressed on those who study his ideals that he refuses to condemn a useful implement merely because it may have been used for wrongful purposes. Though throats have been cut, we do not abolish razors. Though the power made possible by accumulations of capital has been used for oppression, Mr. Coolidge refuses to indict capital by wholesale. He is aware of the misuses of capital, but he is more impressed by the power of capital. He keeps his eye on the truth, that power is necessary for progress. He has a continuous understanding of the almost limitless possibilities for general good in the accumulation and investment of capital. By his familiarity with the history of this country's economic growth he feels that to throw away that mighty potentiality upon which our industrial system has been built would be to make a needless sacrifice, the ill effects of which would be felt not simply by the capitalists, but by all the intricate structure of modern civilization in which capital is an essential factor. Speaking at an Amherst College Alumni dinner in New York City, on November 27, 1920, Mr. Coolidge, then just elected to the vice presidency, made one of his many references to this subject. He said:

"It is not only by technical skill that modern civilization is sustained. It depends to a large degree on accumulated and invested capital, and for its advance will depend more and more on accumulation and investment of capital. Civilization and profits go hand in hand. It is out of the surplus of our efforts that progress is made. It is only necessary to remember the method of conducting all industry, transportation, banking, mining, and commerce, and to observe that they not only need constant renewal but ever-increasing facilities with which to meet enlarged demands, to determine that what we call capital is the chief material minister to the general welfare of all mankind."

He is not holding in mind, in those words, any "special privilege" of a few capitalists. This thought is concerned with the far-reaching benefits made possible by capital rightly used. He is a believer in what is scoffingly referred to by its enemies as "the capitalistic system." He believes in it not as a leverage for exorbitant profits to a few. He believes in it not as a force for selfishness. He believes in it as a steady, dependable, and creative power, making possible profits for the largest number of individuals. Against misuse of it he has often spoken. The right of all the people to share in all the potentialities of our industrial system, stabilized and made secure by our form of government, is in the fabric of all his thoughts. This is, for instance, brought out in his talk before the New

England bankers in New York City, on June 27, 1921. In his remarks at that time he presents both the opportunities of the people and the responsibility of banking institutions in a way typical of his attitude towards banking and its relation to democracy:

"The resources of banks are not the resources of a few rich, but the resources of the people themselves, small perhaps in any individual instance, but, in the aggregate, very large. Nor are banks exclusively a creditor class. It is usually true that they owe to their depositors more than their borrowers owe to them. Every banker knows that to depend on the business and patronage of the rich would be in vain; that if any success attends his efforts, it must be by serving and doing the business of the people. The stock is generally owned by the people, the deposits are always made by the people. This is the reason that banks partake of the nature of a public institution and perform real public service. They are the sole means by which modern commercial activities can be carried on. They afford the method by which the people combine their individual resources, providing a collection of capital sufficient to extend the necessary credit for financing the whole people of the nation.   They hold great power and are under the very gravest responsibilities.   A bank is not a private institution, responsible to itself alone, or to a few.   It is a public institution, under a moral obligation to be administered for the public welfare.   In so far as this standard is accepted and followed, it is my belief that a bank will be prosperous; in so far as it is disregarded, it will be a failure.   Any power which is not used for the general welfare will in the end destroy itself."

In the last sentence quoted a vital portion of Mr. Coolidge's idealism is summed up.   No man could hold a firmer belief in anything than he does in the proposition that unless a power is used for the general welfare, it will ultimately destroy itself.   That thought is the whole substance of his belief in capital; it is the bedrock foundation upon which he places all of our system of banking and finance.   As you read over his speeches and papers, either through

these extracts classified and arranged in this
volume, or by a study of his speeches at length
as they have been published in other volumes,
you will find recurring on page after page this
central thought which may be said to be the
controlling element in his attitude towards every
phase of government, business, and the social
and economic structure of our country. He has
no timid distrust of power. He would use it
for the common good. He says, not only in the
words quoted above but in countless other
places, that nothing can justify itself or continue
in existence for long, unless it is directed towards
a worthy end. He is a firm believer in the futility of selfishness. He is a firm believer in the
omnipotence of service.

Mr. Coolidge undoubtedly has weighed in his
mind the consequences to the banks if the average people refused to use them; and he has
weighed as well the consequence to the people
from such refusal. He sees extending over a
long series of years not simply the financial advantage made possible to large corporations by
a stable and honest banking system, but equally

the advantage of large masses of individuals
served by this same stability and integrity of
our financial structure. He is quite as much
impressed by that service which makes it feasible
for the man of small means to establish a business or to build a home by utilizing the capital
available through the banks, as he is by that
service which makes feasible the growth and
productive capacity of large organizations. To
him all agencies for prosperity and growth are
integral parts of our industrial system ; and
where these come in contact or association with
government he is on the side of those who would
preserve what has operated for the general welfare. He is opposed to those who would tear
down structures which he believes to have
demonstrated their usefulness to such ends. He
has no fear that a misuse of power under our
government can long menace us, because his
study of our history and his knowledge of the
temper of the American people teach him that
such misuse is inevitably self-destructive.

The confidence which he thus shows in capital,
in existing systems of banking and finance, in

the characteristic honesty of American business, in the high ethical levels of the professions — his confidence in all these various manifestations of activity among American individuals traces directly back to this simple assertion; he has an unshakable faith in the people of America. "The American people are sound," he says in one of his recent statements. He knows this to be true. The important thing in his case is, that he not only knows it to be true, but that he predicates all his political actions and all his official procedures upon that proposition. This is not the futile optimism of amiable indifference to existing ills. The faults he sees. He sees them as functional disorders. He refuses to regard them as organic ailments. When he expresses a belief in capital, when he expresses a confidence in the general American banking system, he is manifesting simply his faith in America. He is insistent upon correcting ills; but he is even more insistent on saving the patient's life. He stands firm for the preservation of what he holds to be tested truths.

It is characteristic of Mr. Coolidge that whatever subject he has under consideration, whether it is a basic principle of government or a detail of immediate policy, he looks at both sides and considers them both in whatever he has to say. In his references to capital he sees not only those who hold the capital, but equally those who profit from its uses in the development of industry everywhere. In treating of banks he sees not only the banks themselves as financial institutions, but the great masses of people who, as borrowers, stockholders, or depositors, find their own purposes served by their facilities. Similarly, he sees both sides of the question in his veto of the Bursum pension bill, on May 3, 1924. In this veto he sounds the note for economy. In doing so he emphasizes the thought that money which the government spends it must first take from the people in some form of taxation. In this veto message he says:

"The need for economy in public expenditure at the present time cannot be overestimated. I am for economy. I am against every unnecessary payment of the money of the taxpayers. No public requirement at the present time ranks with the necessity for the reduction of taxation. This result cannot be secured unless those in authority cease to pass laws which increase the permanent cost of government. The burden on the taxpayers must not be increased, it must be decreased. Every proposal for legislation must be considered in the light of this necessity. The cost of commodities is diminishing. Under such conditions the cost of government ought not to be increasing. The welfare of the whole country must be considered. The desire to do justice to pensioners, however great their merit, must be attended by some solicitude to do justice to taxpayers. The advantage of a class cannot be greater than the welfare of the nation."

This is one of the best examples of Mr. Coolidge's vigor of utterance when the occasion demands it. The sentences are short, incisive, abrupt, and unanswerable. They present his intrinsically national comprehension. They are a profession of his trusteeship for all the people of the country. He must stand between the millions of Americans and procedures which would unduly tax them. He sees in every government expenditure not only the thing obtained by such use of government money, but also the strain placed upon those who must furnish the money. He presents the thought that government money is simply money which the government, by its authority, takes from all the people directly or indirectly by taxation. This authority to take money from the people, for whatever purpose, is derived from the people themselves. The moral obligation not to misuse this power, but to protect the people, is ever in this man's mind. There is no aspect of government more important to Americans at this time than this concerning government expenditures. Extravagance in private business is checked by the realization of business executives that failure to check it means eventual bankruptcy. Every head of a business concern watches its finances. He knows that expenditures cannot be made unless the cash is in hand for that purpose, or unless there is a sufficient assurance of ultimate return to warrant borrowing. He knows that money is not made by magic. He knows that receipts and expenditures have a relationship which cannot be negatived by any formula or subterfuge. Business succeeds or fails in accordance with the judgment of those in authority.

It is the peril of all governments that they are tempted, sometimes for good purposes and sometimes from ulterior motives, to authorize or even to encourage expenditures without the slightest regard for the sources from which they are to be met. The business of a government cannot be conducted on a cash basis. It is unavoidable that appropriations shall sometimes be made, or that authorization shall be made for a continuing series of expenditures, considerably in advance of any receipts by which to finance them. The determining factor in decisions of such moment must be, first, the worthiness of the cause served, and, second, the possibility of meeting the cost without imposing excessive burdens upon the taxpayers. The taxpayers pay the bills. They provide the funds which the government expends. Demands upon the government for financial aid are in reality demands by one portion of the public upon all the portions of the public for such aid. It is the way of Mr.

Coolidge not only to keep this plain fact in mind, but in his statements and official papers to present it clearly to the public, as in the veto quoted above.

This concern for the taxpayer, that is, for all rather than for a part of the people, he again exhibits in another veto message, that concerning his return to Congress of the bonus bill unsigned, in May, 1924. In that veto message he says :

"We have no money to bestow upon a class of people that is not taken from the whole people. Our first concern must be the nation as a whole. This outweighs in its importance the consideration of a class and the latter must yield to the former. The one compelling desire and demand of the people to-day, irrespective of party or class, is for the tax relief. . . .

"We have hardly an economic ill to-day which cannot be attributed directly or indirectly to high taxes.

"The prosperity of the nation, which is the prosperity of the people, rests primarily in reducing the existing tax burden. No other action would so encourage business. No other legislative enactment would do so much to relieve agriculture. The drastic executive campaign for economy in government expenditures has but one purpose — that its benefits may accrue to the whole people in the form of reduction in taxes. . . . I cannot recede from this purpose. I am for the interests of the whole people. The expenditures proposed in this bill are against the interests of the whole people. I do not believe they are for the benefit of the veterans. . . .

"The property of the people belongs to the people. To take it from them by taxation cannot be justified except by urgent public necessity. Unless this principle be recognized our country is no longer secure, our people no longer free."

This is no new thought with Mr. Coolidge. As long ago as 1920, when he was the speaker, on June 23, at the commencement of Bates College in Lewiston, Maine, he touched upon this important truth about taxes, saying:

"It is always suggested, when we begin to talk about our economic conditions, that there ought to be some way to make those with large resources pay all the taxes, and I wish that problem were as easy of solution as that; but, unfortunately, it is not, because in the end the taxes have to be paid by the public.   All large incomes are from the public, and when we undertake to say they are for taxation purposes, the result is that they be increased and the public has to pay."

Excessive or unwise taxation is obviously an injustice.   Prodigality in the expenditure of public funds is obviously a deception of the people. The consequences of such expenditure and such taxation are not only unjust, are not only politically dangerous, but, if carried far enough, become utterly destructive economically.   This is the thought found expressed by Mr. Coolidge on several occasions.   In a speech as vice president, on August 15, 1922, at Portland, Oregon, he says:

"There is a very distinct limit to the amount of taxes which can be laid without destroying their source.   Property which is overtaxed disappears.   It is either consumed by taxation, or is forced into some other form."

The distinguishing feature of Mr. Coolidge's allusions to economy and finance, whether he is addressing an association of bankers, a college commencement, a dinner of business men, an association of fellow alumni, or whether he is writing a state paper, is that on each and every occasion he considers such problems in their relation to the welfare of the people as a whole.

CHAPTER XVI

PEACE AND PREPARATION

There are few in the world who prefer war to peace. There are few who would not defend themselves if attacked. One of the problems of statesmen is to maintain national and international peace without the surrender of righteous causes and individual rights. Most men are for peace. The problem consists in devising a method. There is a general agreement as to the end sought. There is a lack of agreement as to the ways by which to approach it.

Amid the perplexities of this problem Mr. Coolidge as President finds himself. It is probable that he will be frequently in contact with them. It is not difficult to forecast his presumable attitude in such matters. Preceding his election as vice president, his public life had not brought him into contact with the subject of international relations, yet he had sufficiently expressed himself to make clear what his attitude would be, and what in fact it now is. Mr. Coolidge, like almost all statesmen, supremely desires international peace. He does not desire it at the cost of the independence or security of his own nation. He has the vision of world peace; but he does not close his eyes to things near at hand. He sees the distant goal; but he sees the immediate pathway no less clearly. He not only knows where he is going, but he takes heed of his footsteps on the way. He sees the limitless aspirations of humanity for peace; and he sees the limitations of human nature. His statesmanship he applies in a practical way. His ideals he holds ever high; but he does not lose contact with the ground.

In the summer of 1924 arose a controversy over the government's plan for observance of September 12 of that year as "Defense Day." Many persons, not only opposed to war, but organized in opposition to it, criticized the government's plan. Anti-war organizations asserted that it was a military gesture. The War Department denied this. The criticism and controversy continued. The National Council for Prevention of War took a leading position in opposition to the proposed "Defense Day"; it asked the President to indorse its three months' campaign for world coöperation to stop war. President Coolidge made this request, and the continuing criticism of Defense Day, the occasion for a letter in which he restated his position concerning the cause of peace and the requirements of national defense. We are not concerned here with this controversy. We are concerned only with Mr. Coolidge's position as stated in the letter dated July 23, 1924. Contained in that letter is this presentation of the President's mind:

"I have been unqualifiedly sympathetic with the aim and purpose to make war, so nearly as might be, an impossibility in this world. Doubtless this is a counsel of perfection not to be realized without much earnest effort; to that, when guided along feasible lines, I have repeatedly pledged my assistance. . . . The Constitution and the law contemplate the maintenance of a defense establishment, which in time of peace always has been and is now, in proportion to our national power and interests, one of the smallest in the world. I have taken an oath to support the Constitution and to execute the laws of the United States. I could do this by maintaining a large standing army. I am opposed to any such plan. I am trying to work out a method by which we can have constantly, as we now have, an exceedingly small army, and leave our citizens free from that burden by letting them assume their own responsibility for a defensive establishment sufficient to provide for domestic peace and order, and national defense.

"Instead of being a military gesture, this plan is the exact opposite. It is a non-militaristic gesture for the purpose of keeping down to its lowest possible point the professional military organization of the United States. Our country has always relied chiefly for its defense upon the readiness of its patriotic manhood to take up arms when necessity presented. After the great military effort of the United States in the World War, our army was demobilized more rapidly and completely than that of any other warring nation."

Continuing the letter, President Coolidge reviews briefly the work of the Washington Conference on Limitation of Armament, and says:

"Our government is compelled to confront the realities of the world. One of these is that international agreement for limitation of armies has not been brought into effect. That being the case, our laws provide a small permanent army and contemplate its expansion to meet emergencies, should they arise. Defense Day is intended to bring to the people a reminder of their relations to, and dependence upon, this skeleton defense establishment, in case our country be attacked. There can be no doubt that failure to prepare for the possibility of war, at a time when that possibility was really imminent, resulted in great hardship, unnecessary expense, and the unjustifiable prolongation of the World War. To state this is but to state what everybody knows.

"It is desirable that both the public officials who would be responsible for the national defense, and the people who would have to make the sacrifices to maintain it, should know something of our plans for it. . . . Profoundly hoping that the outlawing of war from this world may be accomplished, I am yet unable to detect any inconsistency in giving my approval to the program of Defense Day. I wish crime might be abolished, but I would not therefore abolish courts and police protection. I wish war might be made impossible, but I would not leave my country unprotected meanwhile. The defense test seems to me a means to assure the fullest efficiency to the extremely modest defense force our country maintains."

President Coolidge's position as stated in the letter quoted must have been foreseen by any one familiar with his preceding utterances on this subject. As always, he was consistent. In his Memorial Day address at Arlington, on May 30, 1924, he established, or reiterated, his views on the relation between world peace and America's national defense. While he emphasizes on many occasions his belief in the necessity for providing against national helplessness, he

does not omit to couple with this caution the
demand for progress towards a day when all
military establishments throughout the civilized
world shall be sharply reduced and maintained
thereafter at a minimum of strength consistent
with the security of individual nations.   He said
at Arlington :

"It must be remembered that our republic
was organized to avoid and discourage war, and
to promote and establish peace.   It is the leading characteristic of our national holidays that
they are days of peace.   The ways of our people are the ways of peace.   They naturally seek
ways to make peace more secure.

"It is not to be inferred that it would be anything less than courting national disaster to leave
our country barren of defense.   Human nature
is a very constant quality.   While there is justification for hoping and believing that we are
moving towards perfection, it would be idle and
absurd to assume that we have already reached
it.

"We cannot disregard history.   There have
been and will be domestic disorders.

"There have been and will be tendencies of one nation to encroach on another. I believe in the maintenance of an army and a navy, not for aggression, but for defense. Security and order are our most valuable possessions.

"They are cheap at any price. But I am opposed to every kind of military aggrandizement and to all forms of competitive armament. The ideal would be for nations to become parties to mutual covenants limiting their military establishments, and making it obvious that they are not maintained to menace each other. This ideal should be made practical as fast as possible."

In Mr. Coolidge's references to peace and preparation we find him controlled by a process of reasoning which is discernible also as a directing element in his treatment of other matters. He displays not only a faith in American human nature, but an understanding of it. He knows that the average individual American is a peace-loving person, disinclined alike to disorder and to militarism. He can discover no militaristic thought in the mind of America. But he knows also that it is in the nature of Americans to guard their rights jealously. He believes that public opinion in this country will always respond to and support sane movements to diminish not only the menace of war, but all excessive costs in preparation for war conditions. In his mind, as we interpret his writings, he differentiates between what may be called war preparation and what is simply precautionary provision for defense. He is for keeping military equipment within bounds. He is against scrapping the means for defense.

Mr. Coolidge is a student of history. He sees no way by which the future can be assured that the evils of the past need never again be feared. He declines to delude himself with the amiable thought that because we have set our ideals high we can disregard the materialism which in past years has set nation against nation. His program as indicated in his speeches is to keep marching forward towards the ideal of world peace, but in the meantime not to neglect such measures for self-protection as history proves are necessary. In other words, he would by sane procedure preserve for continuing effectiveness those agencies of strength without which no ideals can ever be reached. He sees strength for peace in preparation for emergency. For instance, in August, 1923, he said:

"We want no more war. We want peace with justice and honor. But this does not justify the government in disregarding history, in leaving the people undefended against national peril at home and abroad. Security lies in the realization that a nation has a known force and spirit. To leave a nation unprotected is to be guilty of a crime against the world."

Mr. Coolidge sees consummation of world peace to be, in the last analysis, a matter of human character. By holding the ideal constantly in view, and by refusing to allow destruction to tear down what has already been built, he would have the nation go forward and, little by little, spread in the public consciousness of the world a determination for peace. This thought he indicated in his address to the Associated Press, on April 22, 1924. "We are against war," he said, "because it is destructive.

We are for peace because it is constructive."
Yet he knows that the constructive things of
peace can be destroyed and the whole program
rendered futile by omission to guard against
those destructive forces which still function in
the affairs of men and nations. He sees the
intention of humanity to be good. "We seek
concord," he says, "with all nations through
mutual understanding. We believe in treaties
and covenants and international law as a permanent record for a reliable determination of
action. All these are evidences of a right
intention." Good intentions do not suffice.
Great results are not achieved without them,
but the achievement is the fruit of something
besides intent. Mr. Coolidge sees about him a
practical world. He sees it peopled with men
and women aspiring greatly, but beset by limitations of human nature. He sees everywhere
the growing realization of the hopeless destruc-
tiveness of war, and an increasing determination
to aid in the constructive work of peace. He
sees a growing disposition among the nations to
lay aside the dangerous plaything of military

life and to place their faith in the more durable investment of human character. He sees the binding force of treaties and covenants. He has the lawyer's regard for international law. All these encouragements for the hope of world peace he sees. But he does not let this vision blind him to that which is at hand. In gazing toward the dawn of a new and better day, he does not omit to provide against the journey across distant fields and difficult mountain summits.

Mr. Coolidge's ideals are the guide of his statesmanship. It is his statesmanship which makes them effective.

This need for something more than good intentions he thus summarizes in his Associated Press address:

"But something more than these is required to maintain the peace of the world. In its final determination, it must come from the heart of the people. Unless it abide there, we cannot build for it any artificial lodging place. If the will of the world be evil, there is no artifice by which we can protect the nations from evil results.

"Governments can do much for the betterment of the world. They are the instruments
through which humanity acts in international
relations. Because they cannot do everything,
they must not neglect to do what they can. But
the final establishment of peace, the complete
maintenance of good will toward men, will be
found only in the righteousness of the people of
the earth. Wars will cease when they will that
they shall cease. Peace will reign when they
will that it shall reign."

Development of the idea of peace has the best
chance in the public mind if the nation is best
protected against the danger of destruction.
This we understand to be Mr. Coolidge's
thought.

He makes frequent reference to the potency
of moral power in effecting a physical regeneration in government and among governments.
Its applicability to the problem of world peace
is apparent. This theme appears in his first
message to Congress, in December, 1923:

"The time has come for a more practical use
of moral power, and more reliance upon the prin-

ciple that right makes its own might. Our authority among the nations must be represented by justice and mercy. It is necessary not only to have faith, but to make sacrifices for our faith. The spiritual forces of the world make all its final determinations. It is with these voices that America should speak. Whenever they declare a righteous purpose, there need be no doubt that they will be heard. America has taken her place in the world as a republic — free, independent, powerful. The best service that can be rendered to humanity is the assurance that this place will be maintained."

Mr. Coolidge believes that America stands for something. He believes that it can be most effectively a factor for world peace by maintaining its own physical and political strength. He regards the freedom, independence, and power of this country not simply as a privilege or a benefit enjoyed by its inhabitants, but as a moral force under which those who benefit from it are obligated to act for the welfare of humanity. In pursuit of the goal of world peace he holds important the preservation of what this country stands for

by making secure what this country is. This
doctrine of responsibility appears often in his
utterances. For example, we find it again
expressed in that same message to Congress,
when he makes reference to the Monroe Doctrine.   Here is a very practical American policy,
but Mr. Coolidge sees behind it not only a moral
inspiration but an anticipation of national moral
responsibility.   He says :

"It is one hundred years since our country announced the Monroe Doctrine. This principle has
been ever since, and is now, one of the main
foundations of our foreign relations. It must be
maintained. But in maintaining it we must not
be forgetful that a great change has taken place.
We are no longer a weak nation, thinking mainly
of defense, dreading foreign imposition. We
are great and powerful. New powers bring new
responsibilities. Our duty then was to protect
ourselves. Added to that, our duty now is to
help give stability to the world. We want idealism. We want that vision which lifts men and
nations above themselves. These are virtues
by reason of their own merit. But they must

not be cloistered; they must not be impractical; they must not be ineffective."

By such an interpretation of essentially practical policies, Mr. Coolidge's idealism operates to color and direct his statesmanship. It is the idealism, not of a dreamer, but of a doer.

He has always favored such coöperation among nations as will lessen the menace of war and invite progress toward an enduring peace. In his attitude toward this matter of coöperative progress among nations he brings to bear always his idealistic thought of the purpose in view, his idealistic faith in the essential honesty of the human race, and also his practical knowledge of the limitations of fact, and always his insistence upon the unmenaced integrity of this nation, free, independent, and powerful. In a speech at Fall River, Massachusetts, on April 15, 1919, when he was governor of Massachusetts, he said:

"Whatever covenants or league can be made between the nations, which, without restricting the sovereignty of America or diminishing her power of determining her own affairs, can be

made for the purpose of making war more im-
probable in the future, and peace more secure,
will meet with our support.   This has long been
the attitude of our leading statesmen.   But such
a league must not be a substitute for any other
action for the security of America.   It must be
a supplement to it.   The preparation for defense
by land and sea cannot wait upon it.   The realization that there is still evil in the world which
must be resisted cannot be obliterated by it.   It
is not to take the place of effort, but to call forth
still greater powers in our own people."

Mr. Coolidge is ever for national preparedness.
The preparedness he has in mind takes cognizance of the possibility of war, but is essentially a
preparedness for complete and permanent world
peace.   This goal he sees to be afar off — but
he sees it no less clearly for that.

CHAPTER XVII

THE PROFESSION OF POLITICS

Calvin Coolidge is a politician. If we are to understand his mental processes, it is necessary to keep this fact in mind; but it is equally necessary to understand what we mean by the word "politician." He himself has given us the clue. In his much-quoted address on "The Nature of Politics" he starts out with these words, which have the quality of definition:

"Politics is not an end, but a means. It is not a product, but a process. It is the art of government. Like other values it has its counterfeits. So much emphasis has been put upon the false that the significance of the true has been obscured, and politics has come to convey the meaning of crafty and cunning selfishness, instead of candid and sincere service. The Greek derivation shows the nobler purpose. *Politikos* means 'city-rearing,' 'state-craft.' And when we remember that *city* also meant 'civilization,' the spurious presentment, mean and sordid, drops away and the real figure of the politician, dignified and honorable, a minister to civilization, author and finisher of government, is revealed in its true and dignified proportions."

When Mr. Coolidge says that politics is not an end, but a means, he intends to emphasize not only the negative but the positive. He has a high regard for politics as the means. He sees that there can be no achievement of a functioning democracy without some medium for its operation. An assertion of principles may serve to inspire others, but it has little correlation with the specific tasks in hand unless there is available some practical method by which those principles can be translated into acts. The American Declaration of Independence would have been no more than a dramatic and interesting curiosity of men's emotions and convictions had there not accompanied its production and signing a zeal for action which carries that document into the very forefront of epoch-making papers. The means was at hand to make the Declaration bear fruit. The Constitution of the United States is something more than a well-conceived and cogently expressed formula. It is a cornerstone in the structure of human freedom.   It is so because those provisions which it made for a permanent and authoritative structure were carried out and have continued to operate.   The establishment of national independence for this country, and the creation of an organic law upon which its machinery for self-government has been based, combine to constitute the beginning of a process.   That process is American politics.

Mr. Coolidge calls attention to the fact that, like other values, politics has its counterfeit. We do not destroy precious things because they are imitated by charlatans.   There is a danger to the state in a too wide prevalence of the thought that in the case of politics the counterfeit is typical, and the genuine is rare.   Mr. Coolidge has been for many years in public life. He laid aside the possibilities for self-serving activities and gave himself to the service of government.   This choice he made as a young man.

Through that considerable experience in politics and among politicians, through those years of association with all kinds and classes of politically minded men, he has never lost his faith in the American people, and he has never lost his faith in the politics of the American people. There is a story told of another great politician, Theodore Roosevelt, which is apropos. After his death one who loved him said of him that although he knew more than most men about people, "he still believed in them." A man who knows American politics, and has written what he refers to as his "confessions," is particular to say in his first chapter that his association with politicians through many years has not made him cynical. He believes that the people have more sanity and sense of fair play than they are given credit for; he believes that the intentions of public men are far higher than their critics will admit.

Such an attitude toward politics and politicians will be found to characterize the majority of those who know what they are talking about from actual experience.   Mr. Coolidge certainly has discovered nothing to weaken his faith in the American people, or in their government. That is one of the reasons for his strength. The people have faith in him and he has faith in the people. He does not close his eyes to the presence of dishonesty in politics. In the paper already quoted he says this:

"There are dishonest men in public office. There are quacks, shysters, and charlatans among doctors, lawyers, and clergy, but they are not representative of their professions nor indicative of their methods. Our public men, as a class, are inspired by honorable and patriotic motives, desirous only of a faithful execution of their trust from the executive and legislative branches of the states and nation down to the executives of our towns, who bear the dignified and significant title of selectmen. Public men must expect criticism and be prepared to endure false charges from their opponents. It is a matter of no great concern to them. But public confidence in government is a matter of great concern."

Mr. Coolidge prefers to judge politics by its

best, not by its worst. He simply applies in
politics what the human race inevitably and
always applies, even though subconsciously, to
its affairs. If we were to go through life rating
the profession of law on the basis of its unwor-
thiest manifestations; if we were to judge the
churches by the misbehaviour of those who are
disloyal to them; if we were to cast aside all confidence in business because of the dishonesty of
those who are corrupt; in short, if we were to
condemn all society because of the offenses of
those who miss its significance and fall out of
step, the world would soon slip into such a slough
of despond as would darken the dreams of progress and end all civilization's hopes. The sustaining and propelling force of civilization is
the unconquerable determination of mankind to
judge by the best. Inasmuch as our country will
survive or perish as its government retains or
loses the confidence of the people to whom it
belongs, we need a firmer faith in the essential
decency of politics. We need to apply to politicians the same yardstick which we use in
measuring other men. We need to believe the

simple truth that politics is represented not by
those who demean and debase it, but by those
who exalt and dignify it.

If the people do not have faith in those whom
they elect to office, it must eventually follow
that they will have no faith in one another. A
society in which the people distrust one another
will ultimately breed a situation in which sin-
cerity will have no place. This is a process
of political and social disintegration. The zeal
of the honest man who detects, exposes, and
punishes dishonesty in public office is a mainstay of strength and a guarantee of security
for a republic. We need at all times to guard
against corruption, and we need the services
of unselfish men and women who will devote
their time and their energies to uncovering
that which is sinister and hidden. Respect and
admiration for the art of government, for the
profession of politics, do not counsel protection for the unworthy. On the contrary, it is
more the concern of honest politicians to drive
out the money changers than it is of those less
dangerously associated with them.

Mr. Coolidge by his faith in the people and by his faith in politics has done much to raise the level of politics and to augment — or perhaps to restore — public faith in public men. He sees that the source of government is not on the political summits where holders of high office sit, but is in the homes where political thought is initiated, and whence come the voters who determine the personnel of governing ranks. Again quoting from the same article on the nature of politics, we find him saying:

"Office-holding is the incidental, but the standard of citizenship is the essential. Government does rest upon the opinions of men. Its results rest on their actions. This makes every man a politician whether he will or no. This lays the burden on us all."

When President Coolidge recently informally addressed at the White House a group of women students of the political campaign school conducted by the District of Columbia League of Republican Women Voters, he told them: "If you have come here expecting to find the real seat of power here, I know you will be disappointed, for the seat of power does not rest in Washington — it rests back in those homes that you really represent; and if your coming here is to have any effect, it will be on account of the message that you take back, the inspiration that you receive here which you can reflect in your own homes and in the various communities that you represent." And he advised them: "Take back that message to your co-workers, wherever they may be, to organize themselves for the promotion of sound principles of government."

When we say that Mr. Coolidge believes both in politics and in politicians, we do not imply that he has idealized either the profession or its personnel. He has no misleading illusions. He makes this clear in another portion of his talk to these women at the White House: "I have been in public life for some time, and I learned to say, a long time ago, that I was all through looking for ideal candidates for office. They don't exist, and we have to make the best of what we have, for it is only in that way that we are able to make any progress. Get candidates that are just as near the ideal as possible. That is

what we always want; and after you have done
what you can in the way of selecting a candidate,
do what you can to support the principles which
that candidate represents.   For, after all, if we
are to promote good government, if we are to
promote good principles, it must be by the support of those men and women who represent
those principles."

Mr. Coolidge looks upon politics about as the
normal person looks on other manifestations of
human activity.   He keeps his ideals in regard
to his own profession as most of us keep ours in
regard to that profession or occupation nearest
to us.   The lawyer dreams of the eloquence of
Webster.   The preacher lets his mind dwell upon
the eloquence of Spurgeon or Beecher.   The
writer bows before the shrine of Shakespeare.
The musician pays homage to the memory of
Beethoven.   Politicians hold in their thoughts
the figures of Washington and Lincoln.   It does
not cast them down that they fall short of dupli-
cating the glory of their heroes.   They do not
become cynical because about them they see few
giants.   Their respect is for their profession.   It

has produced a Lincoln. Always it may produce another — just as the law may project another Webster, and as in all walks of life there is ever the allurement of possibility to silence the fears of discouragement.

Abraham Lincoln was a politician before he was a President. Horace Greeley wrote of him when he was first mentioned as a candidate for the presidency, that he was "an adroit politician." And so he was. He did not foresee his name carved in imperishable characters on the scrolls of fame as the savior of the Union. He did not foresee that he would live in history as the great emancipator. He foresaw no details of the vast work he was to do. He set forth from his humble beginning and sought first the practice of law, and next a political office. He might have been called an office-seeker. He must have been and was called a politician. How different, and how less splendid, would have been the history of humanity if Mr. Lincoln in those early days had turned his back on politics and had elected to follow his career as a lawyer in the Western states. Suppose Mr. Lincoln had said to himself: "Politics is a dirty game. Politicians are crooked. I will have nothing to do with it. I will stand on one side and attack politics as the refuge of the corrupt." Mr. Lincoln could not have done that. It would have been a tragedy if he could. He saw politics for what it was. He saw it in truth as the art of government. He saw it as the pathway toward great things — great not for himself, but for his country and for humanity. His career justified his faith, as his faith made possible his career.

Our country's interests are served best by those who see clearest. It was the clear sight of Lincoln that saved the Union. It is the clear sight of Coolidge that strengthens it and steadies it now. This would be impossible but for Mr. Coolidge's faith in the profession of politics.

When President Coolidge addressed the convention of the Daughters of the American Revolution at Washington, in the spring of 1924, he said to them:

"Every voter ought not merely to vote, but to vote under the inspiration of a high purpose to serve the nation. It has been calculated that in most elections only about half of those entitled to vote actually exercise their franchise. What is worse, a considerable part of those who neglect to vote do so because of a curious assumption of superiority to this elementary duty of the citizen. They presume to be rather too good, too exclusive, to soil their hands with the work of politics. Such an attitude cannot too vigorously be condemned. Popular government is facing one of the difficult phases of the perpetual trial to which it always has been and always will be subjected. It needs the support of every element of patriotism, intelligence, and capacity that can be summoned. . . . I am much less concerned for what party, what policies, and what candidates you vote, than that you shall vote, and that your vote shall represent conviction. When an enlightened electorate acts, I have no fear of the result."

In those words of admonition he emphasizes particularly his aversion to any feeling that participation in political affairs can be anything but good. He resents the attitude of those who think themselves "too good for politics."

Mr. Coolidge is a partisan politician. He is a partisan because he believes in the principles of his party and because he believes in the ability of its members. Yet you will find almost invariably when he ventures upon discussion of matters relating to the art of government and the exercise of political privileges and rights, that he lays aside the partisan thought and makes his appeal for respect and support in behalf of American government regardless of party. In such a strain, and in the same speech we have just quoted, he says:

"I do not mean to appeal in behalf of any party. I appeal in behalf of our common country. It is not enough to say that you did not seek the ballot. Your heroic sires did not seek the Revolution. But it came, and they met it by heroic action. Surely the womanhood of the nation, who go down into the valley of the shadow of death for their sons and daughters, cannot long neglect to participate in elections that they and their children may continue to have the advantages of a government that is clean and wise and sound. As it was the initiation of America which made manhood suffrage a modern ideal for the world, so we want now the initiation of America to make citizen suffrage a demonstrated success for the world. I have absolute confidence that if American womanhood will exercise the right of franchise, after fair, considerate, and mature deliberation, voting for what is right as their best judgment shows them the right, that the right will mightily prevail. Surely the womanhood of our country, who have lavished upon the sons and daughters of the land such a wealth of affection, who watch over them in every crisis, from the cradle to the grave, with immeasurable devotion, will not hesitate to make sufficient sacrifice to preserve for themselves and those they love 'the last best hope of the world' — American institutions."

Mr. Coolidge is a politician. He holds the profession of politics high. Maybe it is this faith in his profession that makes him strong in it; and it is certain that something of his own faith he has communicated to the people.

CHAPTER XVIII

Moral Force in Government

At no previous time in our history has so large a proportion of political discussion concerned itself with purely economic problems. Moralists have found texts for sermons in what they interpret as a flagrant materialism; pessimists see in prevailing social tendencies a self-gratification and a disregard for things not physical. Publicists unwittingly strengthen the arguments of these moralists, not by preaching unworthy causes, not by glorifying corruption, but by placing all their emphasis on, and directing all their efforts towards, government problems essentially economic in themselves and under treatment by methods in which the moral argument is omitted. Political tendencies are as materialistic as social tendencies. Even the most progressive leaders focus their thoughts upon cold issues and enlist the arguments of

materialism. We are told by a host of politicians and statesmen that the problems of government are altogether economic. This is not
confined to America. The same over-emphasis
on dollars-and-cents government is discoverable
in other countries. Whether this is a reaction
following the emotionalism of the war, or
whether it would have occurred in any event,
cannot be determined. It is not the cash calculation of corruption, but is rather a conception
of government which eliminates all issues but
those definable by arithmetical figures and formulas.

Therein some statesmen see a fallacy of negation, a blunder by omission. They have in mind
memories of the nation's beginning, as history
records the thoughts and doings of those days.
They are mindful of the fact that in the inception
of this republic there was a moral issue, and
that it was, in fact, a determining issue. They
view with misgivings the inclination towards a
purely materialistic, even though quite honest,
conception of government problems. No man
in public life is more familiar with the specific

needs classifiable under the economic heading
than Mr. Coolidge; but we find him saying, at
Springfield, Massachusetts, on October 11, 1921:

"The foundations of civilization do not rest
alone on economic laws. Human progress must
be paid for, but it cannot be bought. The patri-
cians of declining Rome thought they could protect themselves from uprisings at home and
invasions from abroad with legions filled with
Gauls and Numidians and other barbarian
tribesmen. They found protection could not be
purchased, and beset within and without the
civilization they represented perished. Last
month in a case which almost escaped notice, the
Supreme Judicial Court of Massachusetts
announced a principle of great importance.
'Mere intellectual power,' the decision runs,
'and scientific achievement, without uprightness of character may be more harmful than
ignorance. Highly trained intelligence combined with disregard of the fundamental virtues
is a menace.' America has not sought to purchase protection with mercenaries. When the
call came Americans went themselves. They

did not send.   But there is in our land to-day a great mass yet to be won to the American ways of thought.   Uprightness of character and the fundamental virtues prevail, but the very ease of existence leads many to disregard their laws. Nor is the application of blind justice enough."

And again, in the same address: "Ideals and beliefs determine the whole course of society."

When there has been failure, it has meant that there was no longer sacrifice made to secure success.   Selfishness defeated itself.   That has been the malady of every empire that has fallen, from Babylon to Russia.   Where there has been success it has meant that there sacrifice has prevailed.   That has been the salvation of every people from early civilization to the present day. America was laid in the sacrifices of Pilgrim and Puritan and the colonists of that day.   It was defended by the sacrifices of the Revolutionary period.   It was made all free by the sacrifices of those who followed Lincoln, and is insured by all who accept it.   It was saved by the sacrifices of the World War."

What then is needed now to advance the gov-

ernment toward its goal of perfection? Mr.
Coolidge sees the need to be something more
than precision of intellect. He sees the development of democracy to require something besides
cold intelligence. To him, as we interpret his
writings, the government's requirements are in
a sense analogous to those of the individual. As
man is something more than a machine, so his
government is something more than an assem-
bling of intellects. As man for perfection requires
a soul, so government requires a spirit—expressed
as a moral force. In his message to Congress on
December 6, 1923, he says: "Mere intelligence,
however, is not enough. Enlightenment must
be accompanied by that moral power which is
the product of the home and of religion. Real
education and true welfare for the people rest
inevitably on this foundation, which the government can approve and command, but which the
people themselves must create."

In Chapter XVII we quoted from a talk he
gave to some women at the White House in
which he reminded them that the seat of government was not there, but was back in the homes

they represented.   That thought, which characterizes much of Mr. Coolidge's political philosophy, is again indicated in the quotation above. It is not only necessary, and in fact inevitable, that political authority shall rest with the people, and that they shall initiate and make effective the real reforms and the real progress of the American nation, but it is equally necessary that the inspiration of moral determination shall come from the same source.

This is the true democracy of morality.

It was not by the will of any organized body, or by any individual leader or leaders, that the people in America, at the end of the eighteenth century, determined their course and set about, by severing political ties with the Old World, to set up here a new nation dedicated to the equality of man.   The inspiration for this undertaking, and the moral propulsion which drove it onward, came from the people themselves. Leaders do lead ; but they lead no people against their will.   It is the will of the people which determines history.   If they are materialminded, the achievements of those who represent them in government will lack all but material significance. If they are inspired, those who represent them will record deeds of moral eloquence. Mr. Coolidge reminds us all, as we read his speeches, of his abiding faith in the soundness of the hearts and minds of the people; but what he reminds us of as well is the responsibility which is upon them, and that only as the people have a moral vision and exert a moral will can the courses of government justify the best faith in democracy.

Prominent in the idealism of Calvin Coolidge is his conception of the individual, both as a reservoir and as a propelling force. He encourages in many of his writings the development of the individual through education and hard work. He complements this with the thought that every individual so developed holds his acquisition of learning and experience in trust, and that he can be worthy of what he has only by what he gives. To be well equipped is to be under the heavier obligation to serve society. It is by the moral qualities of the individual that the moral estate of government is determined.

This has always been so. The problems of America to-day, and any day, are the problems of civilized people everywhere and always. Issues and policies differ in detail, as circumstances change. Specific things are required to meet the exigencies of passing moments. But the essential motives of mankind do not change. The need for moral leadership and the need for moral inspiration are inseparable from the constant requirements of all peoples. In his commencement day address at Amherst College, on June 18, 1919, Mr. Coolidge again points to the requirement not only of knowledge, but of its application. He says:

"Civilization depends not only upon the knowledge of the people, but upon the use they make of it. If knowledge be wrongfully used, civilization commits suicide. Broadly speaking, the college is not to educate the individual, but to educate society. The individual may be ignorant and vicious. If society have learning and virtue, that will sustain him. If society lacks learning and virtue, it perishes. Education must give not only power but direction.

It must minister to the whole man or it fails."

If a man, rich in the endowments of a great mind, takes himself into the seclusion of the wilderness and there lives and dies a recluse, shut off from all the rest of the world, he may by himself enjoy a contemplative existence through years of personal happiness; but his mental splendor is of no more value to mankind than though he had not been born. If a man, generously equipped with the accumulations of a well-stored mind, though he lives amid men, omits to apply or to communicate that which he has, he is as much apart from the progress of civilization as though he were a hermit in a hut in the far mountains. Mr. Coolidge preaches a doctrine opposed to mental isolation. He exalts highest that virtue which imparts itself generously.

He knows that knowledge is not always on the side of righteousness. He knows that it may be enlisted in the ranks of evil. That is why he emphasizes so often the need for moral training in the individual; and here his objective is not simply the regeneration of the person, but is also, and more importantly, concerned with society and the state. If there is a moral force characterizing and dominating society in general, the viciousness of one individual may be avoided. If there is no such moral tone in society, the virtue of an individual cannot suffice to preserve a government from disintegration.

Mr. Coolidge's faith leaves no room for pessimism in him. He sees the need for morality in private life and in politics — not simply the technical morality of familiar discussion, but that morality which distinguishes the highest achievements of statesmanship and which leads nations and peoples into the vanguard of civilization's most brilliant marches towards perfection. He has faith that such morality is always present: sometimes militant, assertive, and dominating all things; and sometimes latent, inert, and silent. We discover in his writings a consciousness that this moral factor is never absent, and that even in those periods when it is unheard and appears to be overborne by an aggressive and gross materialism, it is nevertheless present and waiting for the call to bring it forth. It is upon this moral force in society that he counts for the development of a moral force in government. It is by such a moral force in government that he expects the ultimate consummation of a perfect state. He has heeded in thought the tragic as well as the heroic chapters of history. In none of them does he find discouragement. He has balanced the gains and losses, as history records them, and he finds that, reckoned by centuries rather than moments, there has been an upbuilding and a strengthening of the social structure — and that this is so because a moral consideration is always present, even when least asserted. In an address before the American Classical League, at the University of Pennsylvania, on July 7, 1921, he yokes the past and the future together thus :

"We have seen many periods which tried the soul of our republic. We shall see many more. There will be times when efforts will be great and profits will vanish. There have been and will be times when the people will be called upon to make great sacrifices for their country. Unless Americans shall continue to live in something more than the present, to be moved by something more than material gains, they will not be able to respond to these requirements and they will go down as other peoples have gone down before some nation possessed of a greater moral force."

And again, in the same address: "We believe in our republic. We believe in the principles of democracy. We believe in liberty. We believe in order under the established provisions of law. We believe in the promotion of literature and the arts. We believe in the righteous authority of organized government. We believe in patriotism. These beliefs must be supported and strengthened. They are not to be inquired of for gain or profit, though without them all gain and all profit would pass away. They will not be found in the teachings devoted exclusively to commercialism, though without them commerce would not exist. These are the higher things of life."

Mr. Coolidge's faith in the people is at the base

of his whole political career.   He has frequently given it form in words.   One of the most characteristic statements he ever made was this, from his speech to the Massachusetts State Senate, on January 7, 1914:

"We need a broader, firmer, deeper faith in the people — a faith that men desire to do right, that the Commonwealth is founded upon a righteousness which will endure, a reconstructed faith that the final approval of the people is given not to demagogues, slavishly pandering to their selfishness, merchandising with the clamor of the hour, but to statesmen, ministering to their welfare, representing their deep, silent, abiding convictions."

In those lines, as in so many others, we find a confidence in the essential sanity and moral stability of individuals.   He sees the inclination of mankind toward the right.   He sees in men an instinct which teaches them that a government of, by, and for the people must inevitably reflect the best of all people — that this is so even though there come moments in history when less worthy influences may appear for the

moment to have gained the upper hand. He
sees the essential fallacy of demagogues, and he
has that confidence in the sober judgment and
mental balance and moral vigor of the public
which reassures him against any temptation
toward pessimism. He knows by experience
that in the long run the people will turn away
from the quack political doctor and turn to
statesmen whose experience and whose training
are adequate, and whose motives are untainted
by selfishness. He believes in the convictions
in men's minds which, whatever the excitements
and confusions of the hour may be, will infallibly
and in due time lead the people along the safe
highways of honest and efficient democracy.
That is the thought which stands out in many
of his addresses, and which the reader of those
addresses encounters.

Mr. Coolidge's idealism is not an affair of the
distant clouds. Reverencing ideals, he has no
contempt for practical procedures. In his
Wheaton College address, at Norton, Massachusetts, on June 19, 1923, having expressed the
thought that "when the people work out their

own economic and social destiny, they generally reach sound conclusions," he adds

"This is by no means saying that we have reached perfection in any province; it is merely a consideration of some of the things that the liberally educated ought to do to promote progress. We have reached the antithesis of the asceticism of the Middle Ages. There is no tendency now to despise self-gratification or to hold what we call practical affairs in contempt. To adjust the balance of this age we must seek another remedy. We do not need more material development, we need more spiritual development. We do not need more intellectual power, we need more moral power. We do not need more knowledge, we need more character. We do not need more government, we need more culture. We do not need more law, we need more religion. We do not need more of the things that are seen, we need more of the things that are unseen. It is on that side of life that it is desirable to put the emphasis at the present time. If that side be strengthened, the other side will take care of itself. It is that side which is the foundation of all else.   If the foundation be firm, the superstructure will stand."

Mr. Coolidge, as we have pointed out before, does not lose sight of the importance of processes, while he recognizes the importance of objectives. We noted that in his discussion of politics he had regard for politics as the means, although it was a means and not an end.   You will find nowhere in his writings any preachment that "the end justifies the means."   He has a keen eye for the end in view; he has no moments of neglecting to weigh the methods by which the end is to be reached.   They must be always justifiable on their own merits.   Something along this line is the thought expressed in an address by him on April 11, 1916, before the Brockton, Massachusetts, Chamber of Commerce:

"If material rewards be the only measure of success, there is no hope of a peaceful solution of our social questions, for they will never be large enough to satisfy.   But such is not the case.   Men struggle for material success because that is the path, the process, to the development of character.   We ought to demand economic justice, but most of all because it is justice.   We must forever realize that material rewards are limited and in a sense they are only incidental, but the development of character is unlimited and is the only essential.   The measure of success is not the quantity of merchandise, but the quality of manhood which is produced."

In that paragraph he develops the thought of the importance of processes perhaps further than in any other address he has made; for he sets up the hypothesis that objectives themselves are processes.   He paints a broad canvas of humanity upon which it is shown that the achievement of an end much desired may have little value in itself if it does not figure as an item in the continuous development of character.   He sees our own country to have been developed along such lines — objectives won, and then serving as a force by which further and finer objectives are to be sought.   Thus he carries the moral force of government continuously forward.   Material ends may be achieved; they are but incidents in the unremitting development of moral growth.

How necessary he regards such a force in the

affairs of a state is likewise shown in his address
on the birthday of Alexander Hamilton, at
Chicago on January 11, 1922 :

"All the elaborate functions of the government
will be of no avail, unless there abide in the
people the simple, homely virtues of industry
and thrift, honesty and charity. Without these
characteristics there can be no advance in the
general effectiveness of the government or the
general welfare of the people.   All of our natural
resources, all of our attempted industrial organization, all of our guarantees of freedom will
avail nothing without the support of character.
There can be no national greatness which does
not rest upon the personal integrity of the
people."

In his first public speech as President, before
the National Republican Club, in New York,
on February 12, 1924, he cited the instance of
the greatest of all Americans as illustration of
the omnipotence of moral values.   Quotation of
that paragraph here may serve to anchor Mr.
Coolidge's thought relating to moral force in
government :

"In a way all men are great. It is on that
conception that American institutions have been
founded. Perhaps the differences are not so
much as many suppose. Yet there are differences which set off some men above their fellows.
What those differences are in a particular case
is a matter somewhat of personal opinion. To
me the greatness of Lincoln consisted very
largely of a vision by which he saw more clearly
than the men of his time the moral relationship
of things. His great achievement lay in bringing the different elements of his country into a
more truly moral relationship. He was the com-
mander in chief of the greatest armies the world
had then seen. They were victorious. Yet we
do not look upon him as a conqueror. He
directed the raising and expenditure of vast sums
of money. Yet we do not think of him as a
financier. The course which he followed cost
many lives and desolated much territory. Yet
we think of him not as placing a burden on the
nation but removing one from it, not as a
destroyer but a restorer. He was a liberator.
He struck the fetters not only from the bodies

but from the minds of men. He was a great moral force."

What he saw exemplified so greatly in Lincoln he sees reflected and expressed in the American people as a whole. In his address to the Associated Press, on April 22, 1924, he says:

"Fundamentally, America is sound. It has both the power and disposition to maintain itself in a healthy economic and moral condition. But it cannot do this by turning all its thoughts in on itself, or by making its material prosperity its supreme choice. Selfishness is only another name for suicide. A nation that is morally dead will soon be financially dead. The progress of the world rests on courage, honor, and faith. If America wishes to maintain its prosperity, it must maintain its ideals."

Thus he couples with confidence a counsel of warning. He knows that a nation needs to be reminded of its best potentialities. He knows that our prosperity, including that which is purely material, cannot endure if we forsake the moral ideals which are its true inspiration. For honest gain and honest profits he has respect.

We have already quoted him to that effect. For acquisitiveness at the expense of others, for building up a material success upon the ruins of others' chances, for these he has no respect whatever. Let the nation maintain its ideals; then its material achievements will be worthy.

In another speech he says: "If our republic is to be maintained and improved, it will be through the efforts and character of the individual. It will be, first of all, because of the influences which exist in the home, for it is the ideals which are cherished in the home life which make up the strength of the nation."

Thus we come back to the heart of his philosophy of government and character. These things trace to the individual and the home. It is in the home, it is in the hearts of the American people, that we find the true moral force in our government.

CHAPTER XIX

Religion in Government

When Mr. Coolidge took the oath as President, following the death of President Harding, he stood in the living room of his father's house, at Plymouth, Vermont, raised his right hand, and pronounced these words:

"I do solemnly swear that I will faithfully execute the office of President of the United States, and I will to the best of my ability preserve, protect, and defend the Constitution of the United States."

Then, although the Constitution does not require it, he added: "So help me God."

He announced his purpose to carry out the policies which President Harding had begun. In announcing that purpose he added these words: "I have faith that God will direct the destinies of our nation."

Calvin Coolidge shows in countless instances

266

throughout his writings and his speeches a firm faith in God and a strong conviction of the vital part which religion has played in the history of this country. He sees the hand of Divine Providence in all forward movements of civilization in whatever country and at whatever time. This flavor of religion appears in speeches by him on a wide variety of occasions. The thought is always somewhere in his mind. He does not preach; his allusions to religion come easily and naturally. In an address before the Roxbury (Massachusetts) Historical Society, on June 17, 1918, he said:

"The law of progress and civilization is not the law of the jungle. It is not an earthly law, it is a divine law. It does not mean the survival of the fittest, it means the sacrifice of the fittest. Any mother will give her life for her child. Men put the women and children in the lifeboats before they themselves will leave the sinking ship. John Hampden and Nathan Hale did not survive, nor did Lincoln, but Benedict Arnold did. The example above all others takes us back to Jerusalem some nineteen hundred years ago."

He sees as indissolubly joined the finer
instincts in humanity and the responsibility to
divine law. Virtue and religion to him are one.
His is the essential religion found sometimes in
those whose upbringing has been in silent places
amid the grandeur of the works of God. He
does not argue religion; he takes it for granted.
He does not seek for signs; they are ever
present. A wooded hill is for him a gesture of
the Almighty. No less so is the sacrifice of a
mother for her children. The high aspirations
of men are to him the echoes of some divine purpose. In the progress of political ideals he hears
the footsteps of the hosts of an ancient righteousness. He comprehends the foundation of such
a representative democracy, and such a political
system as ours, to be stabilized by religion. Of
our political system he said, before the Evanston
(Illinois) Sunday Afternoon Club, on January
21, 1923:

"It (the American political system) neither
seeks nor claims any justification for its existence
save righteousness. It had its beginning, it
found its inspiration, in the religious beliefs of

the men who settled our country, made it an
independent nation, and established and maintained its Constitution and its laws. If it is to
endure, it will be through the support of men of
like mind and like character."

Impressed as he is by the vigor which attended
the creative period of our country and our
nation, he is equally impressed by the need for a
similar moral strength and a similar sympathy
with religious thought if we are to retain, or to
renew, the authority which characterized those
past years and made their achievements fact.
He sees the necessity always of some religious
flavor in impulses to drive a people or to lead a
people forward and upward. "What are the
sources," he asked, at an Amherst Alumni
Dinner in New York on November 27, 1920,
"of that state of mind which supports civilization? There are but two sources, education
and religion. From them are derived the
teachings of science necessary to give the requisite technical skill and moral ideals sufficient to
support and advance civilization."

This problem of sustaining and advancing

civilization, and the problem of keeping our country vigorous, are referred to by Mr. Coolidge many times. To the consideration of them he yokes usually the thought of religion, as when, at the Memorial Day services in Northampton, Massachusetts, May 30, 1923, he said :

"But if our republic is to be maintained and improved, it will be through the efforts and character of the individual. It will be, first of all, because of the influences which exist in the home, for it is the ideals which prevail in the home life which make up the strength of the nation. The homely virtues must continue to be cultivated. The real dignity, the real nobility of work, must be cherished. It is only through industry that there is any hope for individual development. The viciousness of waste and the value of thrift must continue to be learned and understood. Civilization rests on conservation. To these there must be added religion, education, and obedience to law. These are the foundation of all character in the individual and all hope in the nation."

If Mr. Coolidge sees the unceasing need

for religion in affairs of state, he sees it in no spirit of mourning for a thing lost. He not only has faith in religion, he has faith in the vitality of religion as a factor among men. He does not subscribe to any doctrine of the decline of religious thought. He does not join the chorus of those who bewail what they believe to be the departure of religious significances from the modern works of men. Mr. Coolidge is rather of those who have so firm a belief in the authority of religion, and in mankind's need for its help and for its consolation, that they take it as a matter of course that religion will always operate for the uplifting of the human race. It was on this theme that Mr. Coolidge spoke when he said, in the course of a speech in August, 1923:

"They (religious beliefs) are not a power which is diminishing, but a power which is increasing. The standard of conduct which they require was never before so universally recognized and accepted. It sanctifies every place of worship. It is revealed in every institution of learning, it supports every activity of government, it sustains every economic structure. In domestic affairs, in international affairs, it is more and more the reliance of mankind.

"The evidences of it are increasing, the results of it are increasing. More and more the people are living under the conviction that it is right-eousness alone which exalteth the nation. Surely the recognition of this fact, which stands out above all others, ought to make these days of abiding satisfaction and of continuing faith and determination for the American people."

Mr. Coolidge's regard for religion in its relation to government is an integral part of his Americanism. It has its roots in American history. It goes back even beyond the foun-dation of our nation. In a paper read before the National Geographic Society, on February 2, 1923, and later printed in the *National Geographic Magazine,* he recalls and emphasizes the fact that "the immediate cause of the settle-ment of Massachusetts was a profound religious movement. Green tells us," he continues, "that in the age of Elizabeth England became a country of one book; and that book was the Bible. When the people took that book into their hands, the right of personal judgment in matters of religion became established, and from this there was derived the principle of personal judgment in matters of government. The conclusion of the whole matter was individual liberty."

In that paper we find a point made which he repeats in many other writings. It is the point that an awakened and vital interest in religion both precedes and previsions an assertion of liberty. In his mind he associates religious thought with thoughts of freedom. He traces the beginning of assertive independence back to the time when the people of England had free access to the Bible and made it their book. It is his conclusion that as by such perusal of the Bible they acquired some authority and some confidence of individual judgment in religious matters, so their minds were gradually turned toward individual judgment in matters of government. The brief sentence, "The conclusion of the whole matter was individual liberty," is a concise statement of his deductions from his study of religion in its relation to government.

Among the students of early American history few have so insistently, though not argumentatively, connected religious thought and the growth of freedom. The association of religion and early government on this continent is of course obvious. All have seen it. What Mr. Coolidge does, and what many other students of that period have omitted to do, is not simply to link the religious thought of the time and its accompanying political development as parallel and associated activities, but to connect them as bearing a more vital and significant relation. What Mr. Coolidge sees, as we gather from his frequent references to the subject, is a growth of government beginning and vitalized by a sturdy religious life and thought. He sees the essentially religious nature of our country in the days of its infancy to have been something more than a contributing and casual factor in shaping the events to come. He sees it as an inspiring and propelling force. In his Northampton, Massachusetts, Memorial Day address, on May 30, 1923, he states the case thus:

"It cannot be too often remembered that the

early settlement of our country and the foundation of its institutions was, to a large extent, a
religious movement. They claimed a right of
free choice of religious worship for themselves.
While at first they denied this right to others,
the principle they professed led straight to toleration. They lived in a day that had just discovered, as a result of the Renaissance, the
importance of mankind. It was the beginning
of the end of the slavery of the body and the
slavery of the mind. Out of their religious
beliefs came the conviction that mankind was
born with a right above all others to be free.
This conviction led straight to the right of self-
government. As a necessary corollary there came
the privilege and requirement of education."

To quote once more from his *National Geographic Magazine* article: "What an important
influence the churches and clergymen were in
this early life is apparent wherever we turn. To
Robinson, who remained at home, were joined
others equally prominent who led their flocks to
these shores. As Hooker, the early clergyman of
Cambridge, who, passing on with his congrega-

tion to Hartford, set the inextinguishable mark of freedom and local independence under the representative system upon government, so Shepard, who succeeded to his pulpit and was one of the committee of six magistrates and six clergymen chosen to establish the college, set the same inextinguishable mark upon education. It was in their town that the first book ever printed in America came from the press. Wherever a town meeting is held, wherever a legislature convenes, wherever a schoolhouse is opened, the moral power of these two men is felt. The Puritan was ever intent upon supporting democracy by learning, and the authority of the State by righteousness."

Always he finds at the basis of what may be called the development of American character the motivating force of religious thought and spiritual aspirations. He has not in mind a theocracy or anything approaching thereto. The temper of the early settlers here was antipathetic to any such result. The effect of the strong religious consciousness of the time was not to exalt religion to the exclusion of other influences. It was to erect a form of state in which there would be retained the essential righteousness indicated by sober regard for religious principles. This built not a theocratic state but a democratic state. Its origin antedated the settlement of these shores. In his Y.M.C.A. address at Albany, New York, on April 13, 1923, Mr. Coolidge traces the thread back into history in this manner:

"When we explore the real foundation of our institutions, of their historical development or their logical support, we come very soon to the matter of religious belief. It was the great religious awakening of the sixteenth century that brought about the political awakening of the seventeenth century. The American Revolution was preceded by the great religious revival of the middle of the eighteenth century, which had its effect both in England and in the colonies. When the common people turned to the reading of the Bible, as they did in the Netherlands and in England, when they were stirred by a great revival, as they were in the days of the preaching of Edwards and Whitefield, the way was prepared for William, for Cromwell, and for Washington.   It was because religion gave the people a new importance and a new glory that they demanded a new freedom and a new government. We cannot in our generation reject the cause and retain the result."

In the last sentence quoted Mr. Coolidge ties his interpretation of the past to his understanding of the present and his vision of the future. He regards religion, as the cause of an invigorated sense of individual freedom, to be a consideration still necessary in the minds of those who would correctly gauge present-day problems and who would chart a course amid the uncertainties of the future.   The thesis he presents is that if we are to continue to develop political strength, we cannot afford to ignore moral foundations;   and by moral foundations he means religious foundations.   In another portion of his Y.M.C.A. address just quoted, he states the case in these words:

"America became the common meeting-place of all those streams of people, great and small, who were undertaking to deliver themselves from all kinds of despotism and servitude, and to establish institutions of self-government and freedom. These stupendous results had their source in the great liberal movements of the sixteenth and seventeenth centuries. It was the principle of personal judgment in matters of religion for which the English and Dutch were contending, and which set the common people to reading the Bible. There came to them a new vision of the importance of the individual which brought him into direct contact with the Creator. It was this conception applied to affairs of government that made the people sovereign. It raised up the common man to the place which, heretofore, had been reserved for a privileged class in church and state. It ennobled the people. The logical result of this was the free man, educated in a free school, exercising a free conscience, maintaining a free government. The basis of it all, historically and logically, is religious belief."

In an address on education before the County Teachers' Institute and School Directors' Convention, at Reynoldsville, Pennsylvania, on December 21, 1922, after referring to the emergence of civilization from the Dark Ages, he says:

"But it was not until the great religious revivals of the late Middle Ages that there was laid the foundation for that intellectual awakening which ushered in the modern era of science. The early settlement of New England was a religious movement. Its early government was a religious movement. There was, likewise, a profound spiritual revival in the middle part of the eighteenth century, represented by the teachings and philosophy of Jonathan Edwards and the preaching of Whitefield in the Old World and the New, which preceded the successful assertion of the right of self-government, and which, beginning its triumphant course in America, has never since ceased in its progress."

We might multiply these illustrations of Mr. Coolidge's tracing of the impulses for human freedom back to the religious source; but we have quoted sufficiently to emphasize this line of his thought. That he does not confine his deductions exclusively to the formation of America is indicated in an address delivered by him in Springfield, Massachusetts, on October 11, 1921, in which he says:

"For centuries the church frowned on slavery, though the government legalized it. William the Conqueror drove it out of England; but it was not until 1833 that Parliament outlawed it in the colonies. Through this lapse of time men had turned their thoughts both inward and outward. They discovered themselves, and they discovered humanity. What they discovered the printing press not only recorded in permanent form but diffused among the people. The Revival of Learning, the Reformation, the victory of Oliver Cromwell and the Glorious Revolution, the establishment of American Independence, the French Revolution, and the Reform Bill of 1832, were great movements by the people themselves. At the least they represented a new assertion of moral power, if not a new moral power itself. Henceforth humanity was pitched in a higher register. If the world had produced no greater intellect, it had produced far greater intelligence; if it brought no new moral quality, it brought far greater morality. For the first time the mass of the people, in high places and in low, realized that the moral law was not a mere theory but a practical rule of action. For the first time the people began to live by it, and to require the sanction of its authority. It is this quality which separates present civilization from all that has gone before."

Tracing the thread even further back into history, in addressing the American Classical League, at the University of Pennsylvania, on July 7, 1921, he yokes the intellectual revival of antiquity with religious consciousness, saying:

"The Revival of Learning was the revival of the learning of Greece and Rome plus the teachings of revealed religion. Out of that revival has grown the culture of Western Europe and America. It is important to keep foundations clearly in mind. The superstructure is entirely dependent upon them for support, whatever may be its excellence."

What of to-day? If we believe that there was a cause-and-effect relation between religion and the solution of problems of free government in years gone by, shall we conclude that if we are to solve the problems with us now we must approach them with a due deference to religion? Mr. Coolidge is undoubtedly convinced of the need for such close association. He told the Evanston (Illinois) Sunday Afternoon Club, on January 21, 1923, that "it is altogether natural that those who are connected with religious institutions should be interested in supporting good government. Their interest comes not merely from the ethical teachings of their faith, which are always finally on the side of liberty and justice, established through the maintenance of the orderly processes of the law, but it comes from a realization that in its historical development also religion has laid the foundation of government. This is preëminently true of our American political system."

Somewhat philosophical, and with a suggestion of prophecy, are Mr. Coolidge's words from his Y.M.C.A. speech at Albany, April 13, 1923:

"It is not in the results of a day or a year that the Eternal Purpose is revealed. To judge by such short intervals only would result in being lost in particulars. If we are to avoid being dismayed by the accidental, and if we are to contribute anything, it is necessary to take a larger view, to make a wider survey, and work in harmony with those ever-invincible forces which are always advancing the base-line of progress. No one can tell what a day or a year may bring forth. No one can forecast the fortune of an individual or a township. It may be good or ill. But the evidence is all about of what time and mankind, working together, can accomplish. Both experience and reason give warrant to our faith, both what the past has done and what we know human nature to be. There will be no cause to be disturbed by what is superficial if that which is fundamental remains sound."

Mr. Coolidge's faith in the future is sustained by his knowledge of the past; for in that knowledge is a perspective of the world's spiritual demand. There is a thought for the day in this sentence from his Springfield speech:

"The beliefs for which men have been willing to suffer martyrdom come from religion."

CHAPTER XX

The Gospel of Work

"Satisfaction," says Mr. Coolidge, in an address at the University of Vermont, on June 28, 1920, "does not come from indulgence or satiety; it comes from achievement. Greater liberty does not mean less responsibility, it means more responsibility. That responsibility cannot be borne vicariously; it must be borne by the individual."

Bearing responsibility implies effort and work. Work is the antithesis of selfish indulgence. Work is the doorway to achievement. Liberty is not attained without effort. These are thoughts drawn from a large number of Mr. Coolidge's papers. He preaches the gospel of hard work, whether he is talking to a group of college students, business men, Sunday school associations, patriotic organizations, party political gatherings, or any other assemblage of peo-

ple. He knows work at first hand. His upbringing on 'a Vermont hill farm anchored
within him a consciousness both of the necessity
and of the dignity of toil. In his boyhood days
nothing about him in Plymouth, Vermont, was
obtained except by work. "Special privilege"
does not flourish in New England hill towns.
The strong survive. The weak succumb. The
indolent migrate. All those about Calvin
Coolidge in his boyhood were hard workers.

There is a story of Coolidge's boyhood which
has been often printed but will bear repetition.
It illustrates the attitude of a small boy toward
work. A friend visiting the Coolidge home was
awakened by a noise in the house. Investigat-
ing, she found small Calvin — then nine or ten
years old — bringing wood from the shed into
the kitchen. She called out to him: "Why,
Calvin! Do you know it is two o'clock in the
morning? Why are you doing that at this
hour?"

"I forgot to get the wood in last night, so I
got up to do it now."

There were no push buttons in Plymouth.

There was no way to guide a plow around a field except by hand labor. There was no automatic means for cutting and gathering hay. Wood was chopped by hand. Every item of life for the Coolidge boy was accompanied by the necessity for work. He practiced in his boyhood what the founders of this country practiced when it was a wilderness. He has never forgotten the lessons his experience taught him. Work strengthened his fiber. He likes to work. He believes in work, not only for the achievement of ends, but for the process itself. In 1920, when his friends were active in his behalf at the Republican National Convention in Chicago, he remained at the State House in Boston doing his work as governor of Massachusetts. He was urged to attend the convention. He declined to do so. He did not attend the 1924 Republican convention at Cleveland. He was busy in the White House, doing the work of the presidency.

In July, 1920, at Northampton, his home city in Massachusetts, he received official notification of his nomination as his party's candidate for vice president. The notification speech was made by Governor Morrow of Kentucky. Mr. Coolidge made a brief reply. Mrs. Coolidge and his two boys were present; also his father. After the ceremony was ended, a friend, speaking with Mrs. Coolidge, said she supposed the governor would rest a day or two before going back to Boston. It had been a hard day, with a good deal of ceremony and hot weather.

"No," said Mrs. Coolidge; "Calvin says it is about like any other day. We are going back to Boston to-night." They did. Governor Coolidge was at his desk in the State House at the usual hour the next morning.

The most quoted words of Mr. Coolidge — except perhaps some relating to the Boston police strike — are these, taken from his speech to the Massachusetts State Senate, on January 17, 1914:

"Do the day's work. If it be to protect the rights of the weak, whoever objects, do it. If it be to help a powerful corporation better to serve the people, whatever the opposition, do that. Expect to be called a stand-patter, but don't be a stand-patter. Expect to be called a demagogue, but don't be a demagogue. Don't hesitate to be as revolutionary as science. Don't hesitate to be as reactionary as the multiplication table. Don't expect to build up the weak by pulling down the strong."

This has been called Mr. Coolidge's motto. He has never said it was. He does not work by mottoes; but if he had one, this might serve. It expresses much of his philosophy of government and of life. It reflects something fundamental in his character. In it is a key to his probable courses of action. He has impatience with, or a suspicion of, devices calculated to evade work. He is instinctively averse to plans which shift burdens without due cause. He is for the protection of the weak; but he is against ill-considered panaceas which weaken. He is opposed to any exploitation of the public by privileged power; but he is against persecution of power as such. He is conservative in preserving that which is proved good. He is revolutionary in so far as change constructs, or adds something needed. He is for aiding where aid strengthens. He is against aiding one by the penalization of others. In all these matters a guiding thought in his mind is that which exalts work, and its associate, strength. He knows that work builds. He sees his country building by work, even as work made his country great.

He identifies work with civilization; work in his view is one of civilization's proofs. He is not fond of the expression "hard work." He does not associate work and difficulty. He likes work for its own sake. Here again we find in him a high regard for processes. We work to achieve something, but work is not to be regarded as an obstacle between us and achievement. Work itself is to be desired. It is by acquiring and holding such an attitude toward work that man has advanced from barbarism. Good ends are desirable; but human life cannot be keyed exclusively to the pursuit of ends. Activity is a function of aspiring humanity. This we gather to be Mr. Coolidge's philosophy of labor. He applies it. He likes to work for the sake of work. In addressing the Amherst Alumni Association, on February 4,

1916, he presents a glimpse of this thought. A brief paragraph in that address illustrates what may be called a portion of his idealism. He sees his country facing its problems with a zest for solving them — not simply that they may be solved, but that the minds and characters of the people will be developed and strengthened by effort. Here, as in other manifestations of his ideals, we find an echo of his own early experience, wherein he was brought up to take work as a normal accompaniment of existence, something natural and desirable. In this address he was talking to graduates of his college. He was summoning to service his fellow alumni, in much the same terms he has used in stimulating legislative bodies and others to whom he has talked, or for whom he has written. The concise paragraph is this:

"All growth depends upon activity. Life is manifest only by action. There is no development physically or intellectually without effort, and effort means work. Work is not a curse, it is the prerogative of intelligence, the only means to manhood, and the measure of civilization.

Savages do not work. The growth of a sentiment that despises work is an appeal from civilization to barbarism."

Civilization does not release mankind from toil. The civilized mind looks upon labor not as drudgery, but as life itself. That is Mr. Coolidge's teaching. He is instinctively distrustful of doctrines which have as a portion of their purpose a release from work. There will always be objectives which men will seek. Legislation will not remove them, diminish their number, increase their value, or enhance their attractiveness. Legislation, even though professing pursuit of a particular end, most affects the processes of approaching that end. Proposals to remove all difficulties of process, and to arrive at an end by a short cut in which effort does not figure — these Mr. Coolidge distrusts. He sees the necessity for an unflagging human activity. He sees wise government as a service to the people, but not as a device to make life easy. The savage performed labor because he had to, because he was driven to it, or because self-preservation made it necessary. As he gained civilization and advanced from barbarism, he lightened some of his labors but found the aggregate of work increasing. Those races which found a zest in work advanced fastest and are to-day the strongest. That is the picture which Mr. Coolidge sees in the history of humankind.

He repeatedly directs attention to the futility of the thought that any government can eliminate the need for work. He foresees no social state from which labor is absent. He would regard as doomed to failure any attempted social system which derided or belittled work.

He phrases his thought again, in other words, in his Evanston (Illinois) speech of January 21, 1922, when he says: "The great mistake which is here made is in supposing that under some form of government, or in some advanced state of civilization, people can exist without effort and live wholly at ease. The opposite conclusion would be more nearly correct. It requires less intelligence, less skillful effort, to live among a tribe of savages than to maintain existence under the average conditions of modern society.

Independence, liberty, civilization—these are not easy to bear; they are hard to bear. It is not sloth and ease but work and achievement which are the ideals of the present day. . . . Civilization is the bearer of great gifts, the source of ever-enlarging opportunity. It is not the result of a self-existing plenty, but rather the product of a high endeavor. It does not rob life of all that is noble, but inspires it to all that is heroic."

If civilization has exalted work, if it has inspired humanity to all that is heroic, it has made permanent the requirement for work as a mainstay of its continuance. Mr. Coolidge frequently presents the thought — an obvious thought but one sometimes ignored — that neither freedom nor any kind of civilization is automatic. Individuals exist by activity. States exist by the energy of the people. The capacity and inclination for work make free governments possible. Also they bestow upon the people a continuous interest in life. They operate against that monotony which makes existence unendurable. The desire for progress is instinctive among all normal peoples, but it has its freest play among people who are free. Tyrannies blunt this human desire for advancement. The spirit of tyranny is not a product of despotism; it is what makes despotism sometimes possible. That pernicious purpose seeks its opportunities by devious ways even under democracy. It must always be identified, opposed, and made ineffective. If a people have developed a vigorous activity, and if they have maintained a determination for continuous effort, they need not fear tyranny. Tyranny thrives on the sloth of its intended victims. It is adroit; it profits by the stupidity of others. The weak and complacent succumb to it. The vigorous overthrow it. Workers who have the spirit of work in them do not long submit to tyranny. The lazy and indifferent yield to its seductions, accept its false promise of an easement for their own labors, embrace its offer to shoulder their responsibilities and burdens, and in the end fall into the fetters of slavery. It is some such thought which Mr. Coolidge presents in an address delivered by him, and from which we have already quoted, on June 28, 1920, at the University of Vermont:

"No selfish interest, whatever its source, will long be allowed to interfere with progress. In our economic life as in our political life, progress comes from variety. A division of labor has given to the individual a larger economic existence. But a division of labor presupposes that each division performs its part. By choosing to adopt it the individual imposes upon himself a new duty toward society and receives in return a new economic power and a vastly increased economic liberty. No one denies that he has the right to withdraw, but it is equally clear that he cannot have a right to use his position to levy tribute. Progress and the public welfare do not lie in that direction. The individual is not obliged to make progress. Certainly no one will force it on him. But the American people desire progress, and when they come, as come they must, to a comprehension that all kinds of selfishness and tyranny interfere with it, they will discard their advocates as they discarded the leadership of Toryism, nullification, and secession. After the Almighty had created the first man He blessed him and laid on him the first command to replenish the earth and subdue it. From that time there has been, can be, no escape from the obligation to work. In the subduing of nature man has found character, progress, prosperity, and civilization."

Any reader of Mr. Coolidge's papers will note his respect for history. His considerable reading within the field of politics and economics and American history has given him a foundation for thought, and upon this he has built his structure, and from that structure has raised the banners of his idealism. He sees in historical facts not only the facts themselves, but their significance. He traces in the records of action taken, the motives and the hopes of those who take them. Thus it is that he finds it possible to apply to current problems, and to indicate as policies for the future, that which he has acquired from his study of the past. At a time of many doubts, following the World War, in an address at Carnegie Institute, Pittsburgh, on April 28, 1921, he said this:

"There are readjustments to be accomplished.

There are sacrifices to be made. They cannot
be evaded. They cannot be made vicariously.
They must be made by all the people. It is no
time for bickerings. We must go back to work,
in accordance with the best standard that the
public can maintain, but we must go back
to work. That done, the rest will take care
of itself. Beneath the wrangling, beneath
the tumult, is the sturdy, hard-working, home-
loving American. He decided things in this
country and his decision stands."

Mr. Coolidge sees work not only as the means
for building up a strong state and a strong social
order, but also as the way by which to reassemble
scattered purposes, and to re-establish shaken
structures. "We must go back to work. That
done, the rest will take care of itself." His
knowledge of the past convinces him that where
work controls, mischief may not enter. The old
maxim concerning mischief found for idle hands
he puts in a positive and constructive form. A
busy people, working hard, make progress not
only for themselves but for all.

The need for the gospel of work in the years

immediately following the Armistice was clear
enough. It impressed Mr. Coolidge. It was
in his mind when, on August 2, 1922, he spoke at
an industrial conference at Babson Institute,
Wellesley Hills, Massachusetts. He said:

"During this period (following the war) there
were those who made a wrongful use of their
prosperity. They wasted it in extravagance, or
worse, but they are not representative of the
people as a whole. While they should be
regarded with sympathy, the cause of their condition is perfectly apparent. It is the feeling
of disappointment in the others which is the
cause for concern. If the reason for their discontent be carefully examined, it will be seen
that a considerable part of it is the result of their
not thinking their problem through. They are
the victims, not of the want, but of the deceit-
fulness of riches. They have found that having
power does not remove from them the requirement of effort. They have found that human
existence is not easy, and cannot be made easy.
In whatever station, it is bound to be hard. They
have found that the possession of everything of

value, whether it be liberty or wealth, is held only by meeting the exaction of a price. The greater the value, the greater the price required."

Mr. Coolidge has told boys, as he did a group who called on him at the White House on March 20, 1924, that there "are only two things necessary for boys — hard work and behave themselves"; and he added: "Do that and there won't be any doubt about the future of this country."

Mr. Coolidge believes that a hard-working nation is a straight-thinking nation. He has always worked hard himself. He preaches the gospel of work from the authority of his own experience.

CHAPTER XXI

Thrift and Citizenship

It is not surprising that Calvin Coolidge, born on a New England hill farm and educated in typically New England educational institutions, should have a full realization of the value of thrift. He exemplifies it in his life, he praises it in his speech, he includes it in his political philosophy, and he practices it in public office.

The thrift of the New Englander is instinctive. It is far removed from stinginess. The thrifty man saves but is not miserly. He saves in order that he may use what he has laid by. He saves against the "rainy day" of his own, and to relieve the needs of others. Thrift and charity may go hand in hand. Stinginess and charity are strangers. The New Englander is thrifty; he does not waste. In the regions wherein the Coolidges have lived, at Plymouth, Vermont, sources of supply are few and far between. The country store at Plymouth was in Calvin's youth no great affair. In earlier days of the Coolidge residence at Plymouth there was no store at all. People who live in out-of-the-way places learn to save. Things which city dwellers buy, country-dwellers must make and save. The habit of saving is ingrained. The quality of thrift is deep-rooted in the race. There is an instinctive abhorrence of wastefulness. This quality of saving and thrift Mr. Coolidge has taken with him through his public career. The state of Massachusetts and the nation have profited by it. In three veto messages since he became president he has manifested it. In a veto message when he was governor of Massachusetts, accompanying his return of a bill which would have increased the salaries of members of the Massachusetts Legislature from $1000 to $1500 a year, he said, "It is necessary to decide whether the Commonwealth can well afford this additional tax and whether any public benefit would accrue from it." He further said: "These are times that require careful scrutiny of public expenditure. The burden of taxes resulting from war is heavy. The addition of $142,000 to the expense of the Commonwealth in perpetuity is not to be undertaken but upon proven necessity." He was looking at this proposal through the eyes of New England thrift. He was guarding the Commonwealth against unwarranted expenditure and public waste.

Mr. Coolidge sees the need for private thrift, and he sees the difficulty in impressing that need upon the public consciousness. He knows by his study of history and by his observation of current conditions in his own country that thrift and progress complement each other, and that without one there is little likelihood of the other. In an address before the National Conference of Mutual Savings Banks, at Boston, on April 23, 1920, he said :

"Sometimes it is difficult to get the public to understand not only the necessity but the benefits and the blessings that flow from thrift, industry, and the saving disposition, not only to those who happen to put their money in banks, but to the conduct of all kinds of business enterprises. It is not too much to say that almost the whole of what we call civilization is the difference between saving what we make to-day for use on the morrow, and exhausting it at the time we receive it. And whenever we find a people with sufficient self-control, sufficient balance, sufficient thrift and industry to save their money and increase their capital, there you may be altogether certain that civilization will make progress. Where you find capital being dissipated, where you find a thriftless and improvident population, there you will be equally certain of decline setting in that will end the advance of civilization."

In the same address he presents the contrasting thought that the possession of easily won wealth brings little satisfaction to the possessor, his point, of course, being that the rewards of thrift include not simply a material accumulation, but a stimulating self-respect which is the soundest of all possible bases for contentment and happiness. Mr. Coolidge says:

"We thought that if we could get away from the bread line, and if people could have something of a surplus over what was necessary for their bare existence, they would come into a state of great satisfaction. Some men who have been able to accumulate property could, I think, have testified that such would not be the result, for I never have known a man who has been able to say, because he had acquired a lot of money, he had found all the satisfaction he needed in the world. People in general will have that same experience, and they are disappointed at it. They thought that all they needed was a lot more money and they would be entirely content, and they find that a lot more money is not giving them the satisfaction they expected.

"I think they will have to find their satisfaction, not in indulgence, but rather in achievement, in the fact that they are able to lay by something, and thus in a way increase their power, and in their opportunity to use that power for wise and just ends."

Mr. Coolidge links thrift and citizenship as inseparable comrades. He sees the stabilizing power of possession of property, and he sees that property is not acquired except by the exercise of thrift. It follows naturally enough that the more general the practice of thrift, the more widespread will be the acquisition of real estate and other property, and hence the steadier will be the peace of the nation. In this address to the bankers already quoted he cites proof:

"I recall the serious trouble that broke out in Lawrence (Massachusetts) in 1912, and I knew at that time some of the leaders of the disorder. I recall also the same trouble they had there a year ago (1919). But one of the most remarkable and significant things to me was the fact that some of those who were most violent in 1912 had become prosperous between 1912 and 1919, and had become owners of real estate. They were a strong element for order and security in the community in 1919. That was because they had saved something, and because they had access to the credit of the public, and had been able by that means to make investments. Above and beyond all else, they had made investment in good government, and if you want the support of anybody for anything under the sun, get him to make a slight investment in it, because we have on excellent authority, and it holds true, and will hold true through all the ages, that 'where a man's treasure is, there his heart is also.' If it is for their benefit — and it is for the benefit of everybody if we can make them understand it — that we should have industrial peace, that we should have security for persons and property, then every one will turn in and undertake to support industrial peace, and undertake to support order and peace generally.''

This shows the important place which Mr. Coolidge gives to thrift in his scheme of American citizenship. In another portion of the same address he says :

"Our country is starting out now on certain economic questions, and we never started out in that direction without quite a large number of people getting up and saying that the thing we ought to do first is redistribution of all the property in the nation. It is not of so much importance who happens to own the property as it is that there should be free and easy access to it by those who need to use it. It is of not very great importance to me, if I should want to ride from here to my home in Northampton, so far as my getting to Northampton is concerned, that I should own the conveyance in which I go, or own the railroad. It is a good deal of importance, however, that I should have easy access to the railroad, and because in that collection of invested capital I get the opportunity to ride to Northampton, even at the present rate of fare, at a very great saving to anything that I could do by walking there myself.

"So it is with our money capital. It is very desirable that there should be easy access on the part of the public to the capital of the nation, and that is one of the very best things that our savings banks do. They especially provide credit in our small communities and in rural districts for those who need small credit accommodations to carry on their business. I know that here in Massachusetts our savings banks are not conducted as commercial banks. We recognize that they ought not to be. They are conducted on the whole for the benefit of the public in order that the person of small means who desires to build for himself a home, or purchase a home, may have access to capital and the credit of the community. That is a very great public service, and could not be performed in any way at all without our banking facilities, and the savings banks of our state and nation are doing a great deal to help along that line.

"This is not only a commercial benefit, but it is a benefit to good citizenship, for wherever we can secure in our citizens some interest in the land, the real estate of the community, there you are sure to find a man who takes a sane and reasonable view of things, and who is interested in a wise and economic administration of government affairs."

The thrift of the individual is the thrift of a state. The thrift of a state is the guarantee of its stability. A thrifty people is a law-abiding people. A law-abiding people makes good laws and obeys them. Improvidence corrupts the individual and disintegrates the state. These are the lessons of history. They have impressed Mr. Coolidge. He utilizes many opportunities to impress the people with their truth.

If he is earnest in his counsel in behalf of individual thrift, and if he is impressed by the stability which individual thrift gives to all organized society, he is no less insistent that organized government should practice on a large scale the same virtues which are essential to the welfare of the individual. He has carried with him through all his years of public life this sane conception of the value of generous thrift. As he sees families prospering by such accumulations as are made possible by care and economy, so he sees governments made strong by the exercise of similar economy. It you take the trouble to read his complete veto messages, both as governor of Massachusetts and as President of the United States, you will find repeated at each opportunity the precepts which we have quoted in this chapter. Of thrift and economy in their relation to public affairs he speaks in an address before a meeting of the business organization of the government at Washington, on June 30, 1924:

"We must have no carelessness in our dealings with public property or the expenditure of public money. Such a condition is characteristic either of an undeveloped people or of a decadent civilization. America is neither. It stands out strong and vigorous and mature. We must have an administration which is marked not by the inexperience of youth, or the futility of age, but by the character and ability of maturity. We have had the self-control to put into effect the budget system, to live under it and in accordance with it. It is an accomplishment in the art of self-government of the very highest importance. It means that the American government is not a spendthrift, and that it is not lacking in the force of disposition to organize and administer its finances in a scientific way.

"To maintain this condition puts us constantly on trial. It requires us to demonstrate whether we are weaklings, or whether we have strength of character. It is not too much to say that it is a measure of the power and integrity of the civilization which we represent."

The thought here expressed is much the same as we find in his inaugural address as governor of Massachusetts, January 2, 1919, in which he tells the legislature of his state:

"It is your duty not only to reflect public opinion, but to lead it. Whether we are to enter a new era in Massachusetts depends upon you. The lessons of the war are plain. Can we carry them on into peace? Can we still act on the principle that there is no sacrifice too great to maintain the right? Shall we continue to advocate and practice thrift and industry? Shall we require unswerving loyalty to our country? These are the foundations of all greatness."

Turning to another angle of the same matter, we may take note of his warning against the peril of wastefulness in public expenditure. In that Northampton Memorial Day address from which we have quoted several times he has this to say on the subject:

"There is a very decided limit to the amount which can be raised by taxation without ruinously affecting the people of the country by virtue of confiscation of a part of their past savings. The business of the country, as a whole, is transacted on a small margin of profit. The economic structure is one of great delicacy and sensitiveness. When taxes become too burdensome, either the price of commodities has to be raised to a point at which consumption is so diminished as greatly to curtail production, or so much of the returns from industry is required by the government that production becomes unprofitable and ceases for that reason. In either case there is depression, lack of employment, idleness of investment and wage-earner, with the long line of attendant want and suffering on the part of the people. After order and liberty, economy is one of the highest essentials of a free government. It was in no small degree the unendurable burden of taxation which drove Europe into the Great War. Economy is always a guarantee of peace."

Mr. Coolidge is keenly appreciative of the fact that the only way the government can get money to spend is by taking it from the people in the form of taxation. He knows that every unnecessary public expenditure means an unwarranted reaching into the people's pockets for the money. He knows that there is a direct and unavoidable connection between governmental extravagance and private discontent. An overtaxed people is an unhappy people. It is a truth as old as history. A wasteful government means an overtaxed people. This also is an aged truth. Mr. Coolidge has the advantage of having been trained in a school where thrift was universal, where economy was necessary, and where extravagance was unknown. He has adopted, or rather he has continued, as his political policy precisely the same vigorous principles and habits which have produced the sturdy race from which he sprang. His idealism evisions a nation in which there shall be universal prosperity and a decent contentment under conditions of living which are just to all. What he sees about him now is the unalterable truth that wastefulness in one place means want in another. As the speaker at a dinner of New England Bankers in New York City, on June 27, 1921, he said:

"There can be no permanent prosperity of any class of part. Such a condition can only be secured through a general and public prosperity. This means that to secure this end there must be a general distribution of the rewards of industry.

Wherever this condition is maintained there you have the foundation for an increasing production and a sound financial and economic situation."

The structure of government rests upon the shoulders of citizenship. There can be no strong citizenship but that which is nourished by thrift.

CHAPTER XXII

"The Pursuit of Happiness"

The American Declaration of Independence says: "We hold these truths to be self-evident, that all men are created equal, that they are endowed by their Creator with certain inalienable rights, that among these are life, liberty, and the pursuit of happiness. That to secure these rights, governments are instituted among men, deriving their just powers from the consent of the governed."

The Declaration does not assert that the attainment of happiness is an inalienable right, or that to secure happiness is the purpose of just governments. All that government can do is to guarantee the right to pursue it. This equality of hope we have. The history of civilization is in large part the history of mankind's striving for contentment, of his pursuit of happiness. The pursuit is unending. The goal remains afar.

By devious ways, by varying methods, generation after generation has sought the truth path. It is the problem of states. It is the problem of individuals. No individual has solved it; nor any state.

Through many of Mr. Coolidge's speeches and papers runs the thought of national contentment. Associated with this thought is almost always the thought of work, effort, achievement, and ideals. We gather from his words the thought that happiness is most nearly approximated by those who do not think too closely of it. It comes as the accompaniment of the virtues, as the comrade of labor, as the handmaiden of high thought, as the associate of ideals. In Mr. Coolidge's philosophy little that is worth while comes without effort. Things won cheaply are of scant value. He sees active, and a little menacing, the quality of impatience — the desire to enjoy a harvest without the labor of planting and cultivating. In his talk at Reynoldsville, Pennsylvania, December 21, 1922, before the County Teachers' Institute and School Directors' Convention, he says:

"One of the leading characteristics of modern life is its impatience. People are ambitious to secure the result without being willing to pay the necessary price for its attainment. They want the results of discipline without submitting themselves to be disciplined. They desire the immediate accomplishment of an object which, in reality, can only be secured by a long and laborious process."

Mr. Coolidge has never lost the perspective of the Declaration of Independence. He sees it as a mighty call to effort. In the security of our national life we yield to the temptation to look upon that great document simply as a completed thing. We do not find it easy to put our minds into that condition which must have characterized the minds of those who signed it and those who upheld the signers. We cannot look forward toward a future as those pioneers in free government looked forward to the future immediately before them. We find it difficult to acquire a sense of the physical peril in which they stood, and the moral grandeur of their position. What Mr. Coolidge sees always is the unrelenting necessity for effort if we hope to attain the ends we seek. No object worth while, in his estimation, can be secured otherwise than by a long and laborious process. There is no short cut to education. There is no short cut to national freedom. Sudden actions, acute crises, heroic sacrifices, all these are factors in great chapters of human progress; but they are the high lights, not the whole story. The Declaration of Independence and the act of those who signed it provided drama and inspiration; they did not create a nation. They did not by themselves achieve independence for this country. To establish such independence and to build a nation required sober thought and hard work long continued. The element of effort was the essential thing.

A people's progress toward happiness requires sustained effort as truly as does a nation's establishment of liberty under law. Happiness, in whatever measure it is achieved, must be won, worked for, fought for, paid for. It is not automatic. There is no recipe for it, nor formula.

At Wheaton College, Norton, Massachusetts,

on June 19, 1923, he said : "The satisfactions of
life arise from the art of self-expression.   If these
are not found in the occupational life, they must
be sought and provided from some other source.
Modern industry has its rich compensations.
It not only tremendously increases production,
which on the whole has greatly reduced prices,
placing the necessaries, conveniences, and even
luxuries of life almost within universal reach, but
has very much reduced the required hours of
labor and at the same time greatly increased the
remuneration.   This has provided both the time
and means for the people at large to engage in
outside beneficial and cultural studies and activities.   The American people are nothing if they
are not energetic.   They have accepted these
conditions with their usual enthusiasm and used
their resources in endless effort in an attempt to
provide themselves with amusement, diversion,
and recreation, a considerable part of which
takes the form of lavish expenditure of money
for many purposes which, after a while, are no
longer able to please.   Carried to its logical conclusion, the end is greed and envy."

Mr. Coolidge does not underestimate the material benefits accompanying modern conditions. He draws attention to the "rich compensations" of modern industry. He sees the economic fact that increased production tends to reduce prices and bring within the reach of an increasing number of persons not only the necessaries and conveniences but also the luxuries of life. He is alive to the easing of the physical burden of labor. He takes note of increased remuneration. He sees the lengthened hours of leisure, with their opportunity for self-culture and for amusement. But he sees as well the essential energy of the American people. He sees the feverishness which they apply to the pursuit of amusement. He sees them laboring to rest. He weighs the deceptiveness of money. Such hysterical pursuit of diversion leads to greed and envy. Happiness is not guaranteed by such routes.

Again he touches on this phase of economics and happiness in his Wesleyan University address, on June 21, 1920, in which he says:

"The economic conditions of the eighteenth

century have changed. They were more or less accidental. They will change and change again. They are not the essential elements of our republic. That independence and equality that marked men then is gone, and we have turned, in order that we might facilitate the processes of production and thereby increase its rewards and its benefits, to a division of labor. We have taken men and put them, not into the fields where their occupation changed from day to day and had a varied opportunity for self-direction, and we have harnessed them to the machines and made them, in part, a section or a cog in a machine. This is our industrial question at the present time. Whenever you try to make a machine of a man, it is in his nature to revolt — and they will always do that. We have attempted to solve this question by many and varied expedients. One has been to increase the compensation. I am not now discussing the question of adequate remuneration that ought to go to those who are engaged in our industries. But I think I can lay down this principle, that no man, for any price, will ever

be content to live the life of a machine. And
it won't make any difference what his scale of
compensation will be or may be. He won't find
in that a satisfaction. In fact it is not what we
receive that gives us satisfaction, but what we
give. And it is not in acquisition but in living
the life of men and in achievement that men
find their true and real satisfaction as human
beings. In the early days those who propelled
ships of war were fastened as slaves to the oars
of the galleys. But in our day, those who have
charge of the mechanical power of propulsion
have become officers in the engineers corps,
and they are working now not with their hands
but with their heads. And, after all, you will
find that it is the desire on the part of mankind
to be a head and not a hand. And that is why
I say we can look ultimately to the results of
invention for the solution of some of our
economic questions. We shall have to turn to
the great principle of dealing with men, not on
the question of what they have, but on the question of what they are. Our economic conditions
have changed, but the nature of man has re-

mained constant, and it is in that that we can look for and expect to find a firm and enduring foundation for our republic."

In that address, as in many others, Mr. Coolidge differentiates between the material rewards of life and the greater desires of humanity. He sees the unending rivalry between achievement of material results and the aspiration toward a happiness not to be defined in material terms. He sees the depressing effects, as well as the increased productiveness, of our modern industrial system. How shall we maintain and possibly further increase the physical efficiency of the race and the productive capacity of organized society, and yet not blunt or obstruct the instinctive and ingrained desires of the human race for true contentment? You cannot make a machine of a man. Man is something more than a producer of materials. There is that in human kind which cannot be bound by material restrictions or satisfied by material prosperity. Modern tendencies in industry and in all civilization have been toward development of a high state of machine-like efficiency. They have not eliminated the yearning of the race for other things. Here is our present-day problem. How shall we pursue happiness? Not by a perfected acquisitiveness. We may seek it, says Mr. Coolidge, "in living the life of men." He holds out the hope that modern invention will solve some economic questions — will place new emphasis upon the importance of what men are rather than on what they possess. Economic conditions change; "but the nature of man," says Mr. Coolidge, "has remained constant." To that unchangeable nature of man we must look for the measure of contentment and happiness which is a necessary part in the enduring strength of our republic.

Escape from the privations of poverty is an obvious preliminary to progress towards happiness. But it is a means of pursuit. It does not guarantee happiness. Elimination of all economic distress still might leave the world lacking contentment. National happiness is not negative. At a National Conference of Mutual Savings Banks in Boston on April 23, 1920, Mr. Coolidge said:

"We thought that if we could get away from the bread line, and if people could have something of a surplus over what was necessary for their bare existence, they would come into a state of great satisfaction. Some men who have been able to accumulate property could, I think, have testified that such would not be the result, for I never have known a man who has been able to say, because he had acquired a lot of money, he had found all the satisfaction he needed in the world. People in general will have that same experience, and they are disappointed at it. They thought that all they needed was a lot more money and they would be entirely content, and they find that a lot more money is not giving them the satisfaction they expected.

"I think they will have to find their satisfaction not in indulgence but rather in achievement, in the fact that they are able to lay by something and thus in a way increase their power, and in their opportunity to use that power for wise and just ends."

It is in the use of accumulations, not in the

accumulations themselves, that a promise of contentment lies. Nations and races have had the same experience as individuals. Despots in old days used to resort to such devices as an abundance of feast days and vast public entertainments in the effort to keep the populace amused and thus to keep them satisfied with things as they were. The appeal was entirely to the material appetites of the public. How futile that was is shown by the passing of those old forms of government, by the downfall of tyrants, and by the restless and irresistible march of man seeking freedom. Much of the impetus toward liberty comes from the insatiable demand of men and women for happiness in life. This demand cannot be blunted by efforts to sidetrack them into ways of temporary enjoyment. The liberty of the individual fosters a condition favorable to the pursuit of happiness; and a condition of optimism favored by such pursuit strengthens a people's determination to achieve liberty. On such a theme Mr. Coolidge touches in an address, July 6, 1922, at Fredericksburg, Virginia:

"It is sometimes assumed that Americans care

only for material things, that they are bent only on that kind of success which can be cashed into dollars and cents. That is a very narrow and unintelligent opinion. We have been successful beyond others in great commercial and industrial enterprises because we have been a people of vision. Our prosperity has resulted not by disregarding but by maintaining high ideals. Material resources do not, and cannot, stand alone; they are the product of spiritual resources. It is because America, as a nation, has held fast to the higher things of life, because it has had a faith in mankind which it has dared to put to the test of self-government, because it has believed greatly in honor and truth and righteousness, that a great material prosperity has been added unto it."

Mr. Coolidge sees all about us "this fundamental characteristic of our countrymen." He sees it "in our incomparable charities, in our expanding art and literature, in our philanthropic and patriotic societies, in our tremendous missions, in our religious life. In all these," he says, "there are revealed the fundamental purposes of our people. They are all the expressions of spiritual ideals."

Mr. Coolidge sees the pursuit of happiness, guaranteed under the Declaration as an inalienable right, to be something greater than the building of a material prosperity; indeed, he sees the achievement of material prosperity to be conditional upon a national fidelity to the larger pursuit.

CHAPTER XXIII

EDUCATION

"Education," said Mr. Coolidge, at the Holy Cross College Commencement in June, 1920, "is for the purpose of bringing to bear the experiences of the past in finding the solutions of the problems of the present."

In the preceding chapter we presented a glimpse of Mr. Coolidge's philosophy as it relates to the pursuit of happiness, guaranteed under the American Declaration of Independence as an inalienable right. The subject of the present chapter is akin to it. In the pursuit of happiness, education, Mr. Coolidge believes, is a mighty factor. In his Wesleyan University address on June 21, 1920, he restates, in emphasizing some of the purposes of education, thoughts applicable to the pursuit of human contentment. Looking at history, and at modern conditions, from the angle of education, he said at Wesleyan:

"There is an inherent nobility in mankind that responds to leadership, responds to a presentation of the truth, and responds to a sense of duty. For a man is more than selfishness. He has a desire in him for attainment, and he finds his ultimate satisfaction in the service of his fellow-men. So that, while we may not look ultimately to an increase of compensation, nor for a long time to come to the results of invention and the arts, we can look now and here and forever to the sense of duty that is in our fellow-men to preserve and save ever the foundations of our republic. They will come from the teachings of our institutions of learning and from the teachings of our universities. We cannot re-create the economic conditions of the eighteenth century. We would not desire to do it if we could, because it would not have the power to administer to the economic requirements of the present age. That did its work. That gave to the world what it could in teaching men equality, and went its way with the other great experiences of human kind, and we can't bring it back. But those spiritual foundations, the teaching of philosophy that comes to us in the teachings of Wesley and Edwards — those we can re-create from day to day and from time to time. That is the great work that our higher institutions of learning have to do in the preservation of our state and of our nation."

Education, then, means more than the accumulation of facts. It means more than the absorption of learning. It means equipment for service; and a duty of this service is the preservation of the principles organized and established in our nation. Mr. Coolidge associates education closely with government, that is, he sees in education a clarified comprehension of the purposes of government, and he foresees a stronger state because of educational development. He sees the various efforts of human history contributing, within the limits of their time, to a human understanding of the equality of man. He sees each century, and each generation, carrying onward the responsibility of furthering the rights of man by utilizing the processes of education. Thus he sees upon every institution of learning the burden of

upholding the state. Education, to Mr. Coolidge, is in large measure a bulwark of free
government. This is his conception in a general
sense. In it he is not considering the details of
teaching. He is not, in this attitude toward
schools and universities, holding in mind their
particular classes and courses in the science of
government, or in any of the kindred topics
which have to do with national and social problems. He has in his thought a picture of the
mental development of a race, and of that race's
larger fitness for dealing with problems as they
occur. He is thinking of the soul of education.

Mr. Coolidge has faith in leadership. A
leader is, to him, one whose contact with humanity is close and constant. In his mind leading
and following are closely related. The element
of mutual understanding and mutual trust is
present. He does not class as leader one who
stands apart from, and who regards himself as
above, the masses of people. Leadership and
aloofness have no kinship. The leader must be
close to the ranks. There must be sympathy

between them. The leader must understand those whom he seeks to lead. Those who follow leadership must understand the purposes of him they follow, and must have confidence in his integrity as well as a knowledge of his purposes. It is for such leaders that he looks to school and college. It is in those institutions that he seeks to find both a sympathetic understanding of the problems of the people and an ability to lead toward the betterment of human society. The obligation of education implies such leadership. The obligation upon educational institutions requires its production.

Quoting once more from his Wesleyan University address, we find him emphasizing this leadership, and tracing back its pathway from the beginnings of our republic. He says:

"We are having to look more and more to our universities and colleges and institutions of learning for true leadership and higher inspiration. They were established in New England to be pillars of the state, and there must come out of them leaders and teachers and inspirers of manhood, with a larger vision and a great faith in mankind. We hold by the principles of democracy; but that does not mean that we are to leave the guidance and leadership of those to whom there has come a greater revelation of the truth than has come to some of us. It means that we have a sufficient faith in mankind to believe that they will follow that kind of leadership. And we need it especially now, in order to differentiate between what is accidental and what is essential in the foundation of our republic; for when we can do that, and keep the public mind clearly focused upon what is essential, those foundations are secure and they can never be carried away. A part of what we are goes back to the beginning, of course, of human history; for we are the result of all the experiences of the race. But there comes a time when there have sufficiently developed certain characteristics so that we can say it is the beginning of an era; and the foundation of our republic began back in the middle of the eighteenth century. It was founded in part upon the economic relationship that existed in the colonies in that day. They were without transportation as we understand that term in its modern relationship. They had very little, if any, of a banking system, and the great industrial centers that mark us at the present time were then entirely unknown. Of commerce they had some, but to a large extent they were an agricultural community. That gave them an economic foundation for their equality — for there was very little difference, taking it by and large, between the possessions of those who held the place of authority in those days. So it was altogether a natural thing, economically speaking, that they should declare men were created equal."

A double thought is expressed in that paragraph. He states the need "to look more and more to our universities and colleges" for leadership; he makes clear his comprehension of the obligation upon such institutions to produce it. Educational establishments justify their existence, in his mind, not solely by imparting academic and practical instruction, but in large part also by their continuous contribution to the strength of the state — and by the state he means the people. That is, our educational institutions have a duty to perform in bettering the lot of all the people, including not only those who attend them as pupils, but all others.

It is probable that he believes this thought to have been in the minds of the founders of our republic. He recalls, to these young students at Wesleyan, that these places of learning "were established in New England to be pillars of the state." They were not established to satisfy individual indulgence. They were not established even for the single high purpose of allowing individuals to acquire an education which should benefit them personally and raise their standing in their communities. He sees in retrospect in the pioneer American schools and colleges a willing assumption by them of this thought of the government, and of the leaders of the people, that all such institutions must always contribute strength; also, he believes that some portion of this obligation for public service was knowingly assumed by those who, in those early days of the country, attended such schools. Thus he sees a harmony of democracy and education. He sees the government, school authorities, and all the people acting on the common assumption that the part of education in national development is to benefit all the people all the time. The general understanding of the close relation between education and life he sees to have increased in recent years; also he sees development of some weaknesses. Illuminating is an address at the University of Pennsylvania during his term as vice president:

"Education is undertaken to give a larger comprehension of life. In the last fifty years its scope has been very much broadened. It is scarcely possible to consider it in the light of the individual. It is easy to see that it must be discussed in the light of society. The question for consideration is not what shall be taught to a few individuals. Nor can it be determined by the example of the accomplishments of a few individuals. There have been great men with little of what we call education. There have been small men with a great deal of learning. There has never been a great people who did not possess great learning. . . .

"Perhaps the chief criticism of education and its resulting effect upon the community to-day is superficiality. A generation ago the business man who had made a success without the advantages of a liberal education, sent his son to the university where he took a course in Greek and Latin. On his return home, because he could not immediately take his father's place in the conduct of the business, the conclusion was drawn that his education had been a failure. In order to judge the correctness of this conclusion it would be necessary to know whether the young man had really been educated or whether he had gone through certain prescribed courses in the first place, and, in the second place, whether he finally developed executive ability. It cannot be denied that a superficial knowledge of the classics is only a superficial knowledge. There cannot be expected to be derived from it the ability to think correctly, which is the characteristic of a disciplined mind. Without doubt a superficial study of the classics is of less value than a superficial acquaintance with some of the sciences or a superficial business course.

One of the advantages of the classics as a course of training is that in modern institutions there is little chance of going through them in a superficial way. Another of their advantages is that the master of them lives in something more than the present and thinks of something more than the external problems of the hour, and, after all, it was the study of the classics that produced the glories of the Elizabethan Age with its poets, its philosophers, its artists, its explorers, its soldiers, its statesmen, and its churchmen.

"Education is primarily a means of establishing ideals. Its first great duty is the formation of character, which is the result of heredity and training. This by no means excludes the desirability of an education in the utilities, but is a statement of what education must include if it meet with any success. It is not only because the classical method has been followed in our evolution of culture, but because the study of Greek and Latin is unsurpassed as a method of discipline. Their mastery requires an effort and an application which must be both intense and prolonged. They bring into action all the faculties of observation, understanding, and reason. To become proficient in them is to become possessed of self-control and of intelligence, which are the foundations of all character."

The last paragraph may stand as a condensation of Mr. Coolidge's estimate of the chief purpose of education. It is "a means of establishing ideals"; it must form character; it may properly concern itself with practical matters, but not by that alone can it serve its purpose or justify its continuance. He holds the study of the classic languages to be important; he indicates that frequently. They are important not simply because the acquisition of a knowledge of these tongues may be useful, but because in the exercise of studying them the mind is disciplined and essential faculties are trained. Thus Mr. Coolidge emphasizes education as a process valuable for its own sake, and he sees its result to be something more than an accumulation. It is a means of development and a promise of service.

In an address, on June 28, 1920, at the University of Vermont, on the occasion of his being awarded the honorary degree of LL.D., Mr. Coolidge refers to methods: "There are two methods of education. One is the laboratory or experiment-station method. When problems arise they are sent there, where the methods of exact science are applied and the answer returned. The process is of no consequence; the answer alone is desired. This is the method of authority. Those who drink at that well thirst again.

"Life is not an exact science. In ethics, civics, economics, and politics all the facts are not known. For dealing with these questions we need colleges of the liberal arts to which men go to learn the process for discovering truth. These institutions are established to teach men to think, to create within them a well of water everlasting. This is the justification of that democracy which is the foundation of our republic."

Thus again he places stress upon the power of education to develop, rather than to acquire. He sees education always not as a thing apart, but in its relation to life. As life is not an exact science, so education must be something more than a record of precision. As the problems of government are never completely solved, so we must have active, in the effort to solve them, men and women whose minds remain open, and who have comprehended the meaning of the continuity of existence.

Again referring back to the beginnings of the republic, Mr. Coolidge, in a speech at Springfield, Massachusetts, October 11, 1921, quoted the English historian, John Richard Green, who declared that "in education and political activity New England stood far ahead of its fellow-colonies, for the settlement of the Puritans had been followed at once by the establishment of a system of local schools, which is still the glory of America. 'Every township,' it was enacted, 'after the Lord hath increased them to the number of fifty householders, shall appoint one to teach all children to write and read; and when any town shall increase to the number of one hundred families, they shall set up a grammar school.'"

In comment on this quotation from the historian Mr. Coolidge says: "This clearly states both a fact and a reason. They led in the determination to live by the moral law. That meant freedom. That meant education. For those were the just portion due to that all-important being, man, rediscovered in the new birth of Europe. This was the prologue of that strongest and most permanent of all assertions of the right of men to be free, the Constitution of the United States of America, supported by the determined loyalty of the American people."

Here again we find Mr. Coolidge linking moral character with the political beginnings of the republic; and we find, binding these together, education. We find Mr. Coolidge identifying the spirit in which the early settlers insisted upon educational facilities, with the moral determination of those pioneers. These perceptions by Mr. Coolidge carry further the picture which he constantly presents of a continuous unity which constitutes a large portion of the vigor of the American republic.

While holding these basic opinions of edu-

cation in its relation to government and to moral
life, Mr. Coolidge does not ignore or belittle the
severely practical ends of competent instruction.
He sees the fruits of education applied not only in
those specific fields wherein they are immediately
concerned, but in all details of the life of work.
Such a thought he sets forth in a speech which
he delivered on June 9, 1924, at the annual commencement exercises of Georgetown University:

"The market for trained intelligence will
never be overstocked. We hear of a possible
saturation point in the demand for particular
products; but there will never be a saturation
point, a danger of overproduction, in good, working, capable brains.

"It may be that our educational methods are
not so far perfected as to give us full returns on
all our investments in them. No doubt some
expensive college educations are invested in
people incapable of making them return a going
rate of interest, but that need not greatly worry
us. The world keeps on increasing its wealth
despite a deal of bad investments and sheer
waste. . . .

"The advancement of intelligence has been marked by a continual elimination or amelioration of the more undesirable tasks. Just about the time when it is found that there is a shortage of workers willing to do unpleasant things, somebody with a trained intelligence discovers a process or invents a machine that performs the task more efficiently, or makes its performance unnecessary. This has happened so many times that it seems safe to assume it will keep on happening.

"If there remain some undesirable tasks that neither science nor invention can eliminate, a more productive society will at least be able to pay more liberally — in fact is now doing so — and thus get them done."

Education is far-reaching. Mr. Coolidge sees its contacts with all the affairs of society under a republic. Nor is education, in his conception of it, restricted to the classroom. It enlists the countless opportunities of life for the acquisition of knowledge and for the development of character. He sees all influences which operate to such ends as factors in education. It was that thought which moved him to say in his statement appointing a committee on out-of-door life on April 13, 1924:

"The physical vigor, moral strength, and clean simplicity of mind of the American people can be immeasurably furthered by the properly developed opportunities for the life in the open afforded by our forests, mountains, and waterways. Life in the open is a great character builder. From such life much of the American spirit of freedom springs. Furthering the opportunities of all for such life ranks in the general class with education."

No man can justifiably seek education as a means of self-indulgence, or even for a nobler purpose confined to his own personal ambitions. The obligation upon the educators and the educated is inescapable. By the public comprehension of this the nation makes progress. Mr. Coolidge holds education in such regard.

CHAPTER XXIV

LOOKING FORWARD

How does Calvin Coolidge's philosophy of government provide for the forward look? How does his idealism prepare for the solution of problems ahead? The necessities of the future in any land and under any conditions require a workable political philosophy. Problems differ in detail. They are similar in principle. We are not concerned here, nor have we been in preceding chapters, with the specific matters which must come before him as President. What we are concerned with is his basic thought. We are interested to trace through the quotation of his own words, extending over a period of many years, his sustained attitude toward government and toward society. If we have in any degree illuminated or interpreted accurately his general mental processes, then it should not be difficult in any given instance to have a reasonable assurance of what his probable attitude in that instance will be. In looking forward, then, we are not concerned with the problems of the moment; for these may change. If we have gained an insight into his mind, we will be able to foresee his application to all problems in the future of the same principles of thought and conduct which he has manifested in the past.

In his Memorial Day address at Northampton, Massachusetts, on May 30, 1923, he sounded a word of caution for the future: "A government of the people is not easy to maintain — it is the most difficult of all governments to maintain. Some forget that 'eternal vigilance is the price of liberty.' Some forget the ultimate sufferings and hardships that the people are obliged to bear under an autocratic rule, and turn to it as the easy way. There is scarcely a word in the constitution of any of our states or of the nation that was not written there for the purpose of protecting the liberties of the people from some servitude which a despotic government had at some time imposed upon them."

This caution he offers in no spirit of pessimism.

He gives assurance of safety, requiring only such vigilance as may be looked for in a self-reliant people. The bulwark is the Constitution. To the Daughters of the American Revolution, at Washington, on April 14, 1924, he said:

"We shall succeed if we keep always before us the high purpose which presided at the beginning of our government. We shall need at all times, and we need particularly in this current troubled period, to keep clearly in our thought the conception of our system as the most nearly perfect mode of guaranteeing the essentials of freedom. Under it we have enjoyed liberty without license. Under it we have been saved from the excess of partisanship or of sectionalism. Under it we have grown in strength and wealth and moral authority. But we have never seen, and it is unlikely that we ever shall see, the time when we can safely relax our vigilance and risk our institutions to run themselves under the hand of an active, even though well-intentioned, minority. Abraham Lincoln said that no man is good enough to govern any other man. To that we might add that no minority is good enough to be trusted with the government of a majority. And still further, we shall be wise if we maintain also that no majority can be trusted to be wise enough, and good enough, at all times, to exercise unlimited control over a minority. We need the restraints of a written constitution."

Preservation of the essential integrity of our Constitution Mr. Coolidge sees to be a prerequisite for continued national strength. He regards with suspicion radical changes in that organic law. In his American Bar Association address, at San Francisco, California, on August 10, 1922, he emphasized this caution and repeated his warnings, which we have noted in other chapters, against the mistake of shifting individual burdens upon the state. The people are sovereign; they cannot evade or lay aside the responsibilities of sovereignty. He said:

"One of the proposals for enlarging the present field of legislation has been to give the Congress authority to make valid a proposed law which the Supreme Court had declared was outside the authority granted by the people by the simple device of reënacting it. Such a pro-

vision would make the Congress finally supreme.
In the last resort its powers practically would be
unlimited. This would be to do away with the
great main principle of our written Constitution,
which regards the people as sovereign and the
government as their agent, and would tend to
make the legislative body sovereign and the
people its subjects. It would to an extent substitute for the will of the people, definitely and
permanently expressed in their written Constitution, the changing and uncertain will of the
Congress. That would radically alter our form
of government and take from it its chief guarantee of freedom.

"This enlarging magnitude of legislation, these
continual proposals for changes under which laws
might become very excessive, whether they result from the praiseworthy motive of promoting general reform or whether they reflect the
raising of the general standard of human
relationship, require a new attitude on the part
of the people toward their government. Our
country has adopted this course. The choice
has been made. It could not withdraw now if

it would. But it makes it necessary to guard against the dangers which arise from this new position. It makes it necessary to keep in mind the limitation of what can be accomplished by law. It makes it necessary to adopt a new vigilance. It is not sufficient to secure legislation of this nature and leave it to go alone. It cannot execute itself. Oftentimes it will not be competently administered without the assistance of vigorous support. There must not be permitted any substitution of private will for public authority. There is required a renewed and enlarged determination to secure the observance and enforcement of the law.

"So long as the national government confined itself to providing those fundamentals of liberty, order, and justice for which it was primarily established, its course was reasonably clear and plain. No large amount of revenue was required. No great swarms of public employees were necessary. There was little clash of special interests or different sections, and what there was of this nature consisted not of petty details but of broad principles. There

was time for the consideration of great questions
of policy.   There was an opportunity for mature
deliberation.   What the government undertook
to do it could perform with a fair degree of
accuracy and precision.

"But this has all been changed by embark-
ing on a policy of a general exercise of police
powers, by the public control of much private
enterprise and private conduct, and of furnish-
ing a public supply for much private need.   Here
are these enormous obligations which the people
found they themselves were imperfectly dis-
charging.   They therefore undertook to lay their
burdens on the national government.   Under
this weight the former accuracy of administration broke down.   The government has not at
its disposal a supply of ability, honesty, and
character necessary for the solution of all these
problems, or an executive capacity great enough
for their perfect administration.   Nor is it in
the possession of a wisdom which enables it to
take great enterprises and manage them with no
ground for criticism.   We cannot rid ourselves
of the human element in our affairs by an act of

legislation which places them under the jurisdiction of a public commission.

"The same limit of the law is manifest in
the exercise of the police authority. There can
be no perfect control of personal conduct by
national legislation. Its attempt must be
accompanied with the full expectation of very
many failures. The problem of preventing vice
and crime and of restraining personal and organized selfishness is as old as human experience.
We shall not find for it an immediate and complete solution in an amendment to the federal
Constitution, an act of Congress, or in the find-
ings of a new board or commission. There is
no magic in government not possessed by the
public at large by which these things can be done.
The people cannot divest themselves of their
really great burdens by undertaking to provide
that they shall hereafter be borne by the government."

The guarantees for the future have their roots
in the past. This is not "reaction"; it is evidence of a determination to preserve and apply
that which has been proved true. Mr. Coolidge

faces forward; but he does not forget history.
He sees in all the operations of government the
human equation. He keeps always in mind the
fact that legislation does not and cannot lighten
the responsibility of individual character.
Future problems must be met with a proper
regard for implements which have been always
effective. New problems may require new laws;
but these new laws must deal with old difficulties.
Enactment of a law exerts no magic of automatic
enforcement. Public opinion remains always the
determining factor. The same pressure which
obtains legislation must be exerted to make it
effective as law. This will always be so.

Is there a peril of overcentralization of government? If there is, how shall it be averted?
In an address delivered on April 15, 1924, at the
unveiling of the Arizona Memorial Stone in the
Washington Monument, Mr. Coolidge indicates
the way:

"If we are to maintain the nation and its government institutions with a fair semblance of the
principles on which they were founded, two policies always must be supported.

"First, the principle of local self-government in harmony with the needs of each state. This means that in general the states should not surrender, but retain their own sovereignty, and keep control of their own government. Second, a policy of local reflection of nation-wide public opinion. Each state must shape its course to conform to the generally accepted sanctions of society and to the needs of the nation. It must provide a workable similarity of economic and industrial relations. It must protect the health and provide for the education of its own citizens. This policy is already well recognized in the association of the states for the promotion and adoption of uniform laws. Unless this policy be adopted by the states, interference by the nation cannot be resisted.

"Throughout our whole nation there is an irresistible urge for the maintenance of the highest possible standards of government and society. Unless this sentiment is heeded and observed by appropriate state action, there is always grave danger of an encroachment upon the states by the national government. But it must always be realized that such encroachment is a hazardous undertaking, and should be adopted only as a last resort."

Mr. Coolidge sees federal action as a last resort in instances of local failure. Here, as in many other addresses, he puts emphasis on the need for individual strength. If public opinion everywhere is vitally effective, the appeal for federal action, with its attendant threat of permanent centralization of authority, will not often be made. He has faith in such effectiveness. Speaking at the National Conference of Mutual Savings Banks, in Boston, on April 23, 1920, when he was governor of Massachusetts, he expressed that faith thus:

"I am of a very hopeful disposition, because I believe profoundly in my fellow-men. I said that we were going through a time now of discontent, but I have an abiding faith that out of it we are going to work a condition that will be better than what we have had in the past. These times of discontent are not any reason for discouragement. They are reason for encouragement, and encouragement in every way, because, unless I misread them, they indicate that men are going forward, and no progress is ever made without pain, and no advance ever made without sacrifice. We shall all have to help bear the pain of our fellow-men, and we shall all have to sacrifice part of ourselves for their behalf and for their welfare."

Discontent he sees as a natural manifestation of human nature. It expresses to him a kind of vitality. As a profound student of history, he finds the pathway of civilization marked by the milestones of restlessness. It is a desire for something better which moves men onward, builds nations, and strengthens all humanity. There is a kind of contentment which is sloth. There is a kind of discontent which is aspiration; for it Mr. Coolidge has respect. He does not see it to be a menace, but rather an encouragement. In an address before the Massachusetts Medical Society in Boston, on June 9, 1920, he differentiates between that discontent which is a sign of vitality, and that which is poisonous. In this address he says:

"I am not unaware that there is a certain discontent that pervades all sorts and conditions of society. There is a kind of discontent that ought to be encouraged because it is the foundation of all progress and all advance in human development. There are those that are not contented with the amount of education that they have, and they are therefore applying themselves in our schools and institutions of learning; and that is to the public advantage. There are those that are discontented with their general condition, think that they are not living the lives that they ought to live, and they are changing their methods of life, joining the church perhaps, and determining to live better in the future; that is for the advantage of the public. There are those that think they are not accomplishing enough from their efforts, and they are determining that they will work a little harder in the future and do a little more and produce a little more and be more industrious than they have been in the past; that is a discontent that is for the public welfare. These sources of discontent are discontent with ourselves, and wherever you find that as a condition, you have the foundation

laid for a betterment of mankind. There is another kind of discontent that doesn't look so
encouraging; it is the discontent of those who
want to profit without any effort; it is the discontent of those who want to control without any
ownership, and to rule without legal authority and
responsibility, and in this nation of ours, which
we boast is made up of kings, they want to rule
without being subjects; these are the people that
are discontented with others, and that kind of
discontent isn't one on which you can base any
progress or one on which we can expect the
world to go forward.

"I have sometimes wondered if people would
examine the conditions that are around them,
if they would find really that there was any
reason for great discontent in America. What
is there in our form of government or in our
institutions that men really want to change that
they have not the power to change if they so
will? It is the boast of Americans that here the
people rule and the will of the people is supreme,
and if there is any general reason for making any
change in our governmental affairs and in our

institutions, there is at hand a method of securing it — orderly under the Constitution and according to the laws of the land. I am aware, as you are, that our government is not perfect. The plan of it is fairly perfect, but it is administered by human beings like you and me, and their administration partakes of human infirmities, and that always has been so and always will be so; but that is no reason for undermining the foundation of our institutions or attempting to overthrow our government. Our government is the result of great sacrifice, of long and careful study, and the experience of the intelligence of generations of men. It may be that that ought all to be cast aside; it may be that those who have had no experience with it, who have no background of comprehension of it, can come here from some foreign country and instruct us in the changes that ought to be wrought in it or in the suggestion that it ought to be done away with altogether, but, scientifically looked at, I do not believe that thinking men and women would admit that such was probably the case, and I think there is a disposition on the part of everybody that thinks of these things, to support our government and defend it, come against it what may.

"It is natural for human kind to be discontented with their economic condition. It is especially natural that after a season of great prosperity there should be more discontent in that direction than ever before, because success along that avenue breeds in those who are the recipients of it a desire for greater and greater success, and you have no doubt noticed the phenomenon that as incomes have been increased during the past few years, as wages have risen and risen and risen, instead of bringing satisfaction and contentment to those who have received them, they have had rather the opposite effect of producing a desire for greater and greater increases. That is a natural result, and those who know anything of history say it would be exactly what would happen, but that is no reason for undertaking to overturn our economic system; it is no reason for saying that the relationship on which our economic system is founded ought to be done away with and some

other system substituted for it, because there
again, as in our government, if you look at our
economic system, you will see that nowhere and
at no time has there been such prosperity — material prosperity — as there has been under the
economic system that exists in America. Part
of this discontent is the result of a class consciousness. We recognize no class in America.
There are different conditions and different
stations and different employments. There are
physicians, others may belong to the legal profession, others are engineers, some are manufacturers; but we recognize no condition into
which men are born and to which they are tied
throughout the length of their lives; and any
attempt that is made to mark out and set off
conditions is an entirely artificial and fictitious
designation of the people of America, and any
laws or any institutions or any practices that we
undertake to found upon such a supposition —
that does not work and in the end brings us
disaster."

If there is a contentment which is akin to
sloth, there is a discontent which is but a mani-

festation of laziness. In looking toward the future it is of vital importance that a statesman shall understand this simple fact — simple, but overlooked by the careless and ignored by the demagogue. If a man vested with the authority of political office is to deal intelligently with the tasks of legislation or administration before him, he will have to differentiate in every instance between such manifestations of unrest as indicate a healthy public spirit and a determination to move forward, and those manifestations which are but the evasions of incompetent or slothful ones who expect or desire to live without effort and who would transfer their proper burdens to the shoulders of others. Such a differentiation Mr. Coolidge is peculiarly qualified to make, for his whole political philosophy indicates a pronounced capacity for discrimination among the motives of men. In the address which we have just quoted he makes this clear. In that address also we find the note of optimism which characterizes his utterances generally, and which has a high place in his ideals of government. He would capitalize for the nation's advantage the wholesome unrest of a people surging toward improvement. He would protect the country against the destructive discontent of those unwilling to bear their share of the load.

Evils exist at all times under all governments. They must constantly be attacked. They are a disease of political establishments and must be cured; but more important than the cure is prevention of their recurrence. During the years immediately succeeding the World War there was a set of economic evils, manifested in an exploitation of the public to satisfy the greed of a few, and these demanded treatment. Their cause is of more vital importance than their occurrence. Punishment of the guilty offered insufficient guarantee of future immunity against similar offenses. Mr. Coolidge faces forward. He sees the necessity for protection against recurrent greed. In addressing the Home Market Club in Boston, on May 14, 1920, he said:

"For, after all, profiteering is not so much the cause as the effect of the conditions in which we find ourselves in relation to the prices of our merchandise, and all the laws that you can make

against that pernicious practice won't build a
house for us, won't weave a yard of cloth, or
give our people a single pair of shoes.

"So we shall have to do something more than
punish profiteers in order to secure the result
that your organization is always desirous of
securing. Some of our people in the past few
weeks have taken to wearing overalls. That is
a good idea for a great many of us, but I know
from personal experience that the wearing of
overalls will not solve the problems of the nation
— and, after all, the end of American ideals is
not for the purpose of making a blue-jean nation
out of us. . . .

"It has been suggested that we could do something to relieve ourselves by some means of
taxation. Now there is only one fair requirement for domestic taxation, and that is to provide the means with which the public expenditures may be defrayed. And whenever we seek
by taxation the accomplishment of some other
end than that, we are starting out upon an enterprise that is fraught with great public danger and
an enterprise that will lead no one knows where."

There again he warns against undue reliance upon taxation as a panacea for ills. He sets the measure of future safety upon the foundations of tested methods. Vexation under temporary distress will not lure him into false paths. He insists that the nation's ideals shall be kept high and that the people's pursuit of them shall not be turned aside. He is not misled by quack remedies or by catch phrases of political oratory. Of the call for increased production he says, in his Bates College commencement address in Lewiston, Maine, June 23, 1920:

"We need at the present time, as every one realizes, a greater supply of material resources, a greater supply of food, a greater supply of clothing, and a greater supply of shelter, and the question that is confronting us is, how shall these be secured, how are they to be provided, in order that we may administer properly to the public welfare?

"It is very easy to say that we need to increase production. It is much more easy to say that than it is to secure a remedy of that kind. An increase in production means the gathering to-

gether and the investment of large amounts of
capital, and that means that each and every
individual on the part of the public must practice
the old-fashioned virtue of thrift and economy.
That is the foundation on which to begin. We
need also a general and a better understanding
that the investment of capital in production
gives much more to the public than it does to the
owner of the capital. It is much more for the
benefit of those who buy any of our manufac-
tured articles, or who receive any of the benefits
of our transportation or other commercial enterprises, than it is for those who happen to own
those enterprises when we engage in business
with them. It is much more to the advantage
of the public that the factory should weave for
us a yard of cloth than it is that we should
undertake to weave it for ourselves, or supply
us with transportation than that we should
undertake to supply ourselves with it. That
means that the collection and investment of capital is for the public benefit much more than it is
for the benefit of the owner of the capital, and
the return is less to the owner than it is to the

public. So that it is necessary that we should encourage, by every means possible, the collection, the investment of capital in our industries in order that we may stimulate production."

"Increased production" is not a recipe for the cure of economic ills. It is simply a phrase stating a need. That need can be supplied only by thrift, economy, and effort. Mr. Coolidge, as will have been discovered in earlier chapters, constantly calls upon his countrymen to exercise those qualities. He holds them to be the main source of national strength. By their exercise evils are to be corrected; and by no other way. "Don't expect to build up the weak by pulling down the strong," he once told the Massachusetts State Senate. Mr. Coolidge sees no promise of strength in assaults upon the security of investments — for investments represent not the accumulations of a few persons, but the savings of all the people.

In looking forward with Mr. Coolidge, in undertaking to see with his eyes, in trying to forecast with some degree of accuracy his presumable attitude in relation to problems as yet unspecified, we must take for our guide the record not only of his achievements in office, but of his idealism and his practical statesmanship as expressed in his various speeches and papers. As he himself looks forward, we can imagine him saying now, even as he said on June 28, 1920, when he addressed the University of Vermont upon the occasion of receiving from that institution the honorary degree of LL.D. :

"We have come through adversity. Can we bear prosperity? Are we to turn back toward the cave man who was absolutely free to do as he chose, but yet a slave in all things, or shall we go forward toward the majestic figures of modern civilization who by following duty have found a larger liberty in all things? . . . Go forward in the line of duty, small or great, under discipline, conscious that from doing comes the power to do more, firm in the faith of the fathers, seeking the enlightenment of education, surpassing the hopes of the past, insuring liberty by accepting responsibility, that this whole nation made like-minded with Washington and Lincoln may continue to show forth to the world a revelation of 'the way, the truth, and the light.' "

There will be problems ahead, as there are problems at present, concerning agriculture in our country. These problems Mr. Coolidge will deal with according to their merits. He undoubtedly will apply to them his established doctrine that you cannot magically cure economic ills by legislative short-cuts; but this will not mean abstention from such legislative coöperation and aid as circumstances indicate to be necessary and wise. In speaking, four years ago, on September 30, 1920, at the Great Barrington (Massachusetts) Fair, he had something to say on agriculture which is pertinent now, and will remain so. It is this:

"Agriculture is the basic activity of all mankind. In the nation the yearly value of its products reaches the stupendous sum of $25,000,000,-000, sufficient to pay the national debt. But it is not in its magnitude that it is most important. The importance of agriculture lies in the fact that it is the source of all human activity and the sustainer of all human effort. It replenishes the nation. Without it our country would perish in a day. . . .

"The production of the farm is never interrupted. It never closes down. Unfortunately that is not the case in industry. There is a grave responsibility on those who manage, and those who are employed in industry, in transportation, in mining, to bring their activities up to the farm standard of continuous operation.

"There is nothing our industrial life so needs at present as pacification. We cannot prosper without it. With it we cannot fail. Our whole future is dependent on it, our place in the world abroad, our comfortable circumstances at home. This can be secured by the administration of economic justice so far as possible, and by timely and mutual concessions by all parties in interest when necessary. We need a broader public recognition of these duties. There is before us a prospect the most promising that ever lay before a nation in all history. We can put forth our honest efforts and reap a great reward. We can act the part of economic slackers, of conscienceless profiteers, and reap a corresponding harvest of destruction. The farm of the nation is setting a shining example. Let the rest of the country look at it, appreciate it, and imitate it. And let everybody remember that so long as the farm prospers the nation can prosper, and that when the farm fails the nation fails with it."

Therein he expresses his understanding of the imperative need that agriculture be encouraged by such guarantees as are feasible. He does not underestimate the importance to the nation of this.

In an address before the National Association of Wool Manufacturers, in Boston, on February 11, 1920, he said:

"I am not disturbed about how much money any man makes; I do not believe the government as a general rule ought to be disturbed about that. The thing that disturbs the government is how money is made and what is done with the money that is made. I do not think anybody is too rich or too powerful, but the question comes as to what is being done with riches and power, whether they are being used for the public good or merely used for administering to selfish ends.   I want to suggest to you that you put yourself in the position of using your great prosperity as laying the foundation of administering to the public good."

There again, as so often in his other addresses, he puts emphasis upon the process or method by which things are done; the end sought is not the only consideration in his mind.   The end must be worthy; its worthiness cannot excuse wrongful methods.   He is not alarmed by power; he is insistent that it be exerted in the public's behalf.   Accumulations of wealth do not appear to him to be a menace; the use of such accumulations for selfish purposes is a peril against which he warns.   He holds up three measures of action.   One takes account of the objective; one takes account of the method for achievement; the third embraces the sense of direction.   It is akin to motive.   "It may be of little importance," he told the Brockton (Massachusetts) Chamber of Commerce on April 11, 1916, "to determine at any time just where we are, but it is of the utmost importance to determine whither we are going.   Set the course aright and time must bring mankind to the ultimate goal."

Speaking at the Massachusetts Republican State Convention, in Symphony Hall, Boston, on September 23, 1922, he said:

"Vigilance is always required; discouragement is never justified. The estimation in which the material world holds our country is disclosed by the value which it sets on the American dollar, and the market price of the obligations of our government. But our faith has a more abundant justification. The measure of our country is not found in her material resources. It has a firmer base, a deeper foundation. The true measure of our country is the soul of the American people. Whatever problems press for solution, whatever storms arise, whatever perils threaten our course, we shall rest calm in the assurance that we can appeal to that soul; it will not fail us, it is sound. In it our country is secure."

And in that brief paragraph we find concentrated the essence of the ideals of Calvin Coolidge. He has a firm faith in the soul of his country. Upon it he relies for inspiration and strength. By it he sees the pathway toward a greater material prosperity and a higher spiritual exaltation. To it he will ever appeal with the faith which knows no failure.

CHAPTER XXV

A Speech of Acceptance

On August 14, 1924, in Continental Memorial Hall, Washington, D. C., Calvin Coolidge received formal notification of his nomination by the Republican party as its candidate for President of the United States. He had held this office since August 4, 1923, when he took the oath following the death of President Warren Gamaliel Harding. In his speech accepting the nomination he for the first time stands before his countrymen, addressing them all, in quest of political support for the office of President of the United States. Many of his earlier speeches have been national in scope and application. In this speech of August 14 he is presenting himself to the nation as a candidate for the highest office we have. In this speech we find corroboration of the idealism which has characterized his expressions on occasions cov-

ering many years, and which we have undertaken
to illustrate in the preceding chapters.

With the specification of issues in that speech
we shall not deal.   The detailed problems of the
immediate campaign are not here under discussion.   We have sought in preceding chapters
to reveal the man, and his ideals of citizenship,
through his own words.   By quotation from his
speeches over many years, and by interpretation
of them, we have sought to present the political
philosophy of the President.   We are interested
now in quoting from his speech of acceptance
such portions as reiterate and reëmphasize
points previously made.   The significant fact is
that here, in an essentially political speech as a
candidate for President, he expresses precisely
the same moral and political philosophy that we
have found consistently manifested throughout
his career and throughout his writings.

In Chapter XII we quoted his views concerning the system of party government in a republic.   In the introductory paragraphs of his
acceptance speech he again attests his admiration for that system :

"Very early in their search for a sound method of self-government the American people discovered that the only practical way to secure responsible political action was by the formation of parties, which they adopted because reason pronounced it the most promising, and continued because practice found it the most successful.

"Underneath and upholding political parties was, and is, the enduring principle that a true citizen of a real republic cannot exist as a segregated, unattached fragment of selfishness, but must live as a constituent part of the whole of society, in which he can secure his own welfare only as he secures the welfare of his fellow-men.

"Party means political coöperation, not as an end in itself, but a means, an instrument of government. If founded upon a great moral principle and directed with scrupulous regard for its integrity, it cannot fail to sweep onward and upward, advancing always steadily and surely, a mighty constructive force, a glorious bearer of progress."

Mr. Coolidge's views of the proper relation between government and business we presented in Chapter XIV. Those views are keyed in the thought that Americans are a self-reliant people; that they prosper best under a minimum of governmental interference with their private affairs. Mr. Coolidge's philosophy is one of strength. He applies it in this field. In his acceptance speech he says: "I believe in the American Constitution. I favor the American system of individual enterprise, and I am opposed to any general extension of government ownership and control." And again in this speech:

"We believe the people of the nation should continue to own the property and transact the business of the nation. We harbor no delusions about securing perfection. We know that mankind is finite, and will continue to be under any system. But that system is best which gives the individual the largest freedom of action, and the largest opportunity for honorable accomplishment. Such a system does not tend to the concentration of wealth, but to the diffusion of wealth. Under our institutions there is no limitation on the aspirations a mother may have for her children. That system I pray to continue. This country would not be a land of opportunity, America would not be America, if the people were shackled with government monopolies."

The need for economy in public expenditures is a favorite theme with Mr. Coolidge. He preached and practiced it while a member of the Massachusetts State Legislature, and he has continued to counsel it in every office he has since occupied. This theme we presented in Chapter XV. We find in his speech of acceptance his assertion: "I believe not only in advocating economy in public expenditure, but in its practical application and actual accomplishment." In another portion of this speech he points to the cost of government and pleads for the right of the people to have a larger share of their earnings — this through a reduction of governmental expenses. He says:

"When we come to realize that the yearly expenses of all the governments in this country have reached the stupendous sum of about $7,500,000,000, we get some idea of what this

means. Of this amount about $3,500,000,000
is needed by the national government, and the
remainder by local governments. Such a sum
is difficult to comprehend. It represents all
the pay of 5,000,000 wage-earners receiving $5
a day, working 300 days in the year. If the
government should add on $100,000,000 of
expense, it would represent four days more work
of these wage-earners. These are some of the
reasons why I want to cut down public
expense.

"I want the people of America to be able to
work less for the government and more for themselves. I want them to have the rewards of
their own industry. That is the chief meaning
of freedom. Until we can reëstablish a condition under which the earnings of the people
can be kept by the people, we are bound to suffer
a very distinct curtailment of our liberty."

Continuing to emphasize the drain upon private pockets by governmental expenditure, he
points out the primary demand which taxation
makes upon the individual. This is a striking
paragraph :

"These results are not fanciful, they are not imaginary; they are grimly actual and real, reaching into every household in the land. They take from each home annually an average of over $300. And taxes must be paid. They are not a voluntary contribution to be met out of surplus earnings. They are a stern necessity. They come first. It is only out of what is left after they are paid that the necessities of food, clothing, and shelter can be provided, the comforts of home secured, or the yearnings of the soul for a broader and more abundant life gratified. When the government effects a new economy, it grants everybody a life pension with which to raise the standard of existence. It increases the value of everybody's property and raises the scale of everybody's wages. One of the greatest favors that can be bestowed upon the American people is economy in government."

Discussion of a foreign policy is inevitably present in any political campaign in any country in these years since the World War. Mr. Coolidge treats the subject in his acceptance speech, and in doing so again manifests the attitude which we have undertaken to interpret in Chapter XVI. He is enthusiastically eager for an enduring world peace. He is unwilling to leave his country unprepared for emergencies. In his acceptance speech he summarizes the essential foreign policy of the nation thus:

"The foreign policy of America can best be described by one word — peace. Our actions have always proclaimed our peaceful desires, but never more evidently than now. We covet no territory; we support no threatening military array; we harbor no hostile intent. We have pursued, are pursuing, and shall continue to pursue with untiring devotion the cause of peace. . . . Our country has always been against aggressive war and for permanent peace. Those who are working out detailed plans to present such a policy for consideration have my entire sympathy. I trust that never again will the women of this nation be called on to sacrifice their loved ones to the terrible scourge of war."

In many of the earlier chapters of this book Mr. Coolidge's sympathetic regard for the rights and the common cause of all the people has been made manifest by quotations from him. We find the same attitude expressed in this paragraph of his acceptance speech :

"The domestic affairs of our country appear to me to be by far the chief concern. From that source comes our strength. The home market consumes nearly all of our production. Within our own boundaries will be determined to a very large degree the economic welfare and the moral worth of the American people. These are plain facts, but there are others equally plain."

And in another portion of the speech :

"The federal government ought to be, and is, solicitous for the welfare of every one of its inhabitants, every one of its business activities, whether they be small or great. This is one country; we are one people united by common interests. There should be no favorites and no outcasts; no race or religious prejudices in government. America opposes special privilege for anybody, and favors equal opportunity for everybody. It has adopted these principles because they are the logical conclusions of our ideals of freedom. Moreover, we believe they

contribute to our material welfare. We oppose
the artificial supports of privilege and monopoly
because they are both unjust and uneconomic.
They are not right. They do not work. No
sound and enduring government or prosperity
can rest upon anything but the sure foundations
of equal opportunity and justice for all."

An echo of Mr. Coolidge's frequent inclusion
of religious thought in political discussion appears in this reference to peace: "We believe
in the brotherhood of man, because we believe
in the fatherhood of God. That is our justification for freedom and equality." The associated
idea of moral force in government, treated in
Chapter XVIII, appears in his latest speech
thus:

"We believe in the law of service, which
teaches us that we can improve ourselves only
by helping others. We know that these principles are applicable alike to our domestic and
our foreign relations. We cannot live unto ourselves alone."

If there must be economy in public expenditure, there must likewise be thrift in private

management. These requirements earlier chapters have emphasized. Applying the principle to the conditions following the war, Mr. Coolidge in his acceptance speech says:

"The war left us with many evils. One result was the tremendous wastage of wealth. The people of this country were required to re-create very nearly one fifth of our national resources. All of this stupendous sum has to be earned. When so large a part of the work of three hundred years is swept away, it is not easily recovered. It takes all the tremendous energy of men, of enterprise, of the vast properties represented by invested capital, and of material, working through years, to repair the damage and replace the values destroyed by war.

"The only method by which we can make up this loss is by saving a part of what we produce each day. It will make little difference how much we raise on the farm, or how much we turn out in the mill, if it is all used up or all the proceeds are expended. We can only be relieved of our present private and public burdens by refraining from private and public extravagance. We must resist private and public outlays for which there is no commensurate return. This is economy. Whatever anybody may claim or say, there is no other method by which the people can rid themselves of their tremendous financial burdens."

That Mr. Coolidge as President retains undimmed his appreciation of the rights of the people he discloses in these words:

"The government of the United States represents the public. It is its business to protect and advance the general welfare. It wants every one treated fairly, and expects every one to do his duty. It must be impartial, but it ought to be humane. It wants to establish justice, equity, and mercy. It desires to see adequate returns both for capital invested and for work done. It believes in protecting health and in cherishing education. It is opposed to the domination of either wealth or organized minorities, and is committed to the free rule of all the people."

Mr. Coolidge carries forward in office that

progressive conservatism which he has consistently preached and practiced through his career hitherto. In accepting the presidential nomination, at a time when there is much discussion of radical ideas, he says:

"We are likely to hear a great deal of discussion about liberal thought and progressive action. It is well for the country to have liberality in thought and progress in action, but its greatest asset is common sense. In the commonplace things of life lies the strength of the nation. It is not in brilliant conceptions and strokes of genius that we shall find the chief reliance of our country, but in the home, in the school, and in religion. America will continue to defend these shrines. Every evil force that seeks to desecrate or destroy them will find that a Higher Power has endowed the people with an inherent spirit of resistance. The people know the difference between pretense and reality. They want to be told the truth. They want to be trusted. They want a chance to work out their own material and spiritual salvation. The people want a government of common sense."

As one studies and reviews Mr. Coolidge's speeches extending over the period of his public life, the most striking feature encountered is a rigorous consistency. There is no flavor of opportunism in Mr. Coolidge's political thought. He has a definitely conceived and logically maintained philosophy of life. He applies it to all questions. That is why we find in the speech in which he accepts the nomination for President of the United States an application of his frequently expressed principles to the issues immediately before him. And that is why, if one studies with care this philosophy of his, one should not find it difficult to forecast with reasonable accuracy his presumable courses of action. The public subconsciously knows this to be so. It is possibly the basis for its confidence in him.